THE THREE MARRIAGE

ENIGMAS

The Secret Reasons Marriages Fail and
How to Ensure Your Marriage Survives

KEVIN FOSTER

Discovery Path Publishing

ISBN: 978-0-9974429-0-8

Library of Congress Control Number: 2016937802
Discovery Path Publishing, Elkhart, IN

Discovery Path Publishing
1623 Garden Street
Elkhart, IN 46514

DEDICATION

To my Sweet Paula, for her never-ending love and support. Her wisdom, devotion, and help have been nothing short of inspirational.

To Pastor Matthew Pieters, without whose persistence and encouragement I would have never written this book.

ACKNOWLEDGEMENTS

I am very grateful for the people who assisted in the writing of this book.

First, I would like to thank Kevin Miller, my editor. His expertise and knowledge have transformed my poorly written manuscript into the wonderful book you now hold. His experience, insightfulness, and ideas were wonderful.

I would also like to thank Cindy France and Pastor Matthew Peters, whose challenging questions and comments helped mold and shape parts of this book.

Also Pastor Tim Revis, whose scholarly advice helped balance what is and is not important.

And finally, Randy Foster, whose insight on bringing it all together was incredible.

CONTENTS

INTRODUCTION

Connie and Mike have fallen madly in love. Mike can't imagine life without Connie, so he asks her to marry him. Connie is thrilled, because Mike is the man of her dreams. The courtship has been magical, and both are ecstatic about getting married. Four years later, disappointed and heartbroken, Connie files for a divorce. What happened to their beautiful love together?

Jim and Rhonda have been married for thirty years. They are happy—well, fairly happy. They love each other a great deal, and they seldom argue. They have learned to live together and become good friends, but there's little romance or intimacy between them. Why not?

Sam and Becky have been married for seventeen years. Their marriage has little love or intimacy, and they are fairly hard on each other, yet they're unwilling to get a divorce. Sam has been having an affair for over two years, but Becky is clueless about it. Both believe they are destined to live like this for the rest of their lives. What happened to their love for each other?

Ron and Penny have been married for eleven years. They are happy together and believe their marriage is pretty good. There were some hard times, but now their daily routine has settled down, and life seems good for the most part. Both would love more intimacy together, yet it seems to elude them. They don't make love as often as Ron would like, but they see friends with marriages that are far worse and feel lucky just to have the happiness that they do. Neither Ron nor Penny understands why they cannot have the marriage of which they always dreamed.

These marriages all face the same underlying problem: Somewhere along the way, their intimacy was destroyed, and without it, the marriage failed, even if the couple never got divorced. As widespread as such difficulties are, the problems that sabotage intimacy are invisible, *enigmas*. Just about every couple faces these same enigmas. If not dealt with properly, they can lead to what I call the "downward spiral in marriage." Worse, these enigmas interact with and feed on each other, which makes them even more difficult to identify and eliminate. Rather than being in control, most couples are struggling and helpless, because they are unaware the enigmas exist, much less how to overcome them. It is the great heartache and pain that millions suffer during marriage and after divorce that has inspired me to write this book. I understand their pain from personal experience, and my heart breaks for these people.

Investigating the Crash Site

When an aircraft goes down, a team of investigators with expertise in different fields rushes in to determine the cause of the crash. Such investigations are extensive and can take months or years. Even with experienced investigators studying the crash, sometimes they still come away with questions for which they have no answers. These are *enigmas*, circumstances or events that are mysterious, puzzling, and difficult to understand.

In marriage, we also encounter enigmas that can cause a relationship to crash and burn. However, unlike a plane crash, when a couple divorces, no team of expert investigators rushes in to discover the cause. Instead, spouses end up blaming each other, because they have no idea what actually occurred.

I have spent a great deal of time studying this area, and I believe this book will help you identify the hidden enigmas that destroy intimacy in marriage and then show you how to prevent them from sending your marriage into a nosedive even if you and/or your spouse have already hit the ejection button.

I believe that most issues in marriage are solvable if the marriage is built with the right ingredients and the couple is committed toward building an intimate relationship with each other. If you and your spouse understand and are dedicated to meeting each other's needs, wants, and desires, you can overcome these enigmas and go on to enjoy an intimate, affair-proof marriage.

What Qualifies Me to Write This Book?

As a pastor, I have counseled many couples. It was heart-wrenching to watch them suffer. But it was only after suffering the pain of divorce myself and then searching for answers that I believe God revealed the truth to me about why so many marriages fail—and how to avoid that fate.

I know what it is like to be married and yet feel extremely lonely. I know how it feels to be married and yet live a life of celibacy for years, having only friendship but not intimacy with your spouse. I know the devastating feeling in your heart when your spouse asks for a divorce and what it feels like to lose a life partner of thirty years. I understand the emotions that well up within you when you have to face your first holidays without your spouse and the tremendous pain you suffer from the loss of family.

My search for truth began long before my divorce, but unfortunately, I didn't discover the answers in time. However, even after my divorce, I continued my search until all of the pieces finally came together. I spent countless hours fasting and praying, seeking God's face and begging for wisdom and answers. I also read many books and articles in search of answers. Most importantly, I never gave up. As a result, I believe God has revealed these enigmas to me and, more importantly, how to overcome them.

Many people, especially Christians, treat divorce as an unforgivable sin and believe that it disqualifies someone from offering marital advice. After all, why would we take advice on marriage from someone who has failed at it?

Point taken. However, consider this: Is it any wiser to take advice from someone who has never been divorced but who has an unhappy marriage? Of course not, and yet people in unhappy marriages dispense marital advice daily. I attended a marriage seminar once led by a couple who had written a book on marriage, and by the end of the seminar, they were arguing and attacking each other verbally. Needless to say, I did not buy their book.

I define a happy marriage as a relationship with intimacy and joy at the core. How many marriage counselors can claim such credentials? I have seen many couples who have been married over fifty years who are miserable, but at least they stuck it out! Sorry, but I don't need or want their advice either. Some might believe staying together like that is noble, but I would not care to spend one year in such a relationship just to be able to boast about how long I had been married.

Something else I find incredible is the small number of couples with long marriages who actually have a high degree of joy and intimacy but have no idea why they are different. As a result, they have little advice to offer others despite their happiness.

The truth is, people who have never reached the end of their rope are clueless about how to advise someone who has. The same goes for those who have been to the end of their rope but never figured out how to climb back up.

Thankfully, God doesn't require perfect knowledge or experience from those he calls to lead or teach. More important than either of the above qualifications is a willing heart. In the Bible, God often chooses and uses the person we would least expect to teach or lead others. God chose a shepherd boy, David, to be the king of Israel. On one occasion, he even chose a donkey to reveal the truth to someone.

Perhaps I am not so far from that donkey, but I hope you will agree that this book serves as proof that people who have been divorced can still offer sound marital advice. My discoveries and conclusions are the result of personal experience, trial, error, emotional pain, study, prayer, and revelation. I trust that this book will prove itself by revealing the hidden problems that sabotage intimacy and then provide simple, although not simplistic solutions.

Despite my confidence in the material this book contains, please understand that there are limits. This book deals with problematic marriages, not problematic people. If your spouse is narcissistic, a sociopath, bipolar, abusive, has a gambling problem or drug or alcohol addiction, I recommend seeking professional counseling and/or reading *Desperate Marriages* by Gary Chapman.

Finally, in case you haven't guessed already, let me also state clearly that I am a Christian. As such, I make biblical references in this book for my Christian brothers and sisters. However, the information in this book is universal and can be used by everyone regardless of their faith position to help create a spectacular marriage.

Understanding This Book

I make several general statements in this book. They should be understood as just that, generalizations. Rarely are my statements about men or women absolute. There are exceptions, because every individual is different. That being said, the exceptions are a small percentage.

One of the things I have discovered is that men and women share traits, but each sex generally dominates in certain areas. When I say, "men are this way" or "women are like that," there is about a 70/30 percent split, give or take a few points. For instance, when I say men are visually-oriented, we definitely are, but a hunky-looking man is eye candy for women as well. This is a good example to remember. Certain people may find themselves reversed in the percentages. Every blanket statement I make falls under this general percentage equation, so keep that in mind while reading this book.

I am not trying to reinvent the wheel here. When other authors have covered a subject and done a good job of it, I will cite examples from their books and give them credit for their work. Some of the better books on marriage I have read include:

- *His Needs, Her Needs: Building an Affair-Proof Marriage* by Willard F. Harley, Jr.
- *The Proper Care and Feeding of Husbands* by Dr. Laura Schlessinger
- *For Women Only* by Shaunti Feldhahn
- *The Five Love Languages* by Gary Chapman

Each of these books brings fresh information about marriage and helps people to have happier marital relationships.

Apart from these books, a body of work is also becoming universally known that is covered in several books. In the pages that follow, I will consider that work public domain.

This book is divided into two sections. The first eight chapters are dedicated to understanding the enigmas and how they interact to destroy intimacy. The remaining chapters explain how to overcome these enigmas and restore your marriage to a place of unbridled joy and intimacy.

I should also warn you that this book contains bold, frank, and what some may consider "mature" information. I have tried to tone things down somewhat, but there are limits. Some facts might surprise you as we deal with the truth. Since infidelity is the most common cause of divorce, we are going to dig deep into the hidden facts about sex and affairs in marriage. Unless you understand these truths, your marriage will be vulnerable to an affair.

Finally, this is not a "feel good" book. It is an "identification of the problems and solutions" book, which will help you understand marriage relationships. I don't just want you to have a happier marriage; I want your marriage to be the dream you believed marriage could be. Yes, your marriage can be wonderful if both you and your spouse want it to be. Are you ready to make that happen? Then let's get started!

1

THE PROBLEM

Think of your marriage as a two-engine aircraft. An aircraft stays aloft due in part to its engines, which propels it through the sky. This is equivalent to your marriage's level of intimacy. Intimacy is the result of the amount of love (fuel) flowing into your hearts (engines) and propelling your marriage (the aircraft) through the air. The amount of thrust your heart produces is a product of how much love your spouse injects into it and vice versa. The depth of intimacy (altitude) your marriage attains is a direct result of this thrust from both engines.

If an aircraft's engines do not receive enough fuel, the engines will sputter and maybe even stall, causing the aircraft to lose altitude and possibly crash. The aircraft may even go into a downward spiral, sending it spinning out of control as it dives toward the ground.

When an aircraft is caught in a downward spiral, applying thrust alone is not enough to help it recover. In fact, it can actually make things worse. Instead, what is required is the knowledge and ability to handle the aircraft, especially during times of crisis.

The same is true of marriage. If your heart does not receive enough love from your spouse, your relationship will sputter and stall. In addition, when your marriage begins to lose altitude, merely loving your partner is not enough. You need to know how your partner works so you can understand how to apply your love in the correct way, especially during a crisis situation.

Sometimes pilots have no idea the aircraft is going to stall, so aircraft have been fitted with stall warning sensors that caution the pilot to take remedial action. Marriage isn't quite so simple. Often married people have no clue their marriage has stalled out and that they are in a downward spiral, never mind how it happened or what they can do about it. Rather than take control of their relationship, like a plane in a flat spin, their relationship takes control of them.

Some spouses react by hitting the eject button and bailing out. Other couples are able to level off at a low altitude, just skimming the treetops, but they are still in danger of crashing. Still others wait until things are so bad that they crash and burn. And just like a real plane crash, the loss of your marriage can cost you your life!

No Greater Pain

Divorce is an incredibly painful experience. Many people join divorce support groups to cope with the pain they are experiencing. Some who are in the midst of this pain believe it will never end. Their lives are shattered, and most of them have no idea why. A little research on the subject shows that divorce pain resembles grief over the death of a loved one. Divorce can reach deeper though, because it affects things outside of the marriage. It can sabotage friendships as well as relationships at work. I believe divorce can be the greatest loss a person ever suffers.

In fact, the only common link to suicide in the United States and Europe is divorce. A recent study by the National Institute for Healthcare Research in Rockville, MD reports that divorced men are three times more likely to commit suicide.[1] The study also shows that divorce is the number one factor in suicide overall. A study by the European regional office of the World Health Organization studied European countries and found divorce was the only common factor for suicide among all thirteen member nations.[2] The divorced person's pain becomes so great that it feels unbearable. These people don't believe their pain will ever improve. When someone feels despair and believes that the pain will not end, he or she is at a high risk for suicide. Far too often, we even hear of murder-suicides.

Even when married, some people are so lonely and desperate for love that they turn to affairs for comfort. Rather than make things better though, affairs just make things worse. In fact, the number one way marriages end is in affairs.

---

[1] "A Prioritized Research Agenda for Suicide Prevention," Action Alliance for Suicide Prevention, accessed January 20, 2016, http://actionallianceforsuicideprevention.org/sites/actionallianceforsuicide prevention.org/files/Agenda.pdf

[2] "Preventing Suicide: A Global Imperative," World Health Organization, accessed January 20, 2016, http://apps.who.int/iris/bitstream/10665/131056/1/9789241564779_eng.p df

Statistics show that women usually give up and want out of the marriage first. Divorce Lawyer Source brings together what limited studies have been conducted, by the National Center for Health Statistics and the American Law and Economics Review. They list these sources and present this information on their website.[3] The studies reveal women file for the majority of divorces—up to ninety-percent for college-educated couples. Sometimes a woman may have her husband file, but often it is at her request. After reading this, I began questioning divorced women about who filed for divorce, her or her ex-husband, and sure enough, my unscientific poll mimicked the scientific ones.

I wrote this book for both men and women, but in truth, it is directed more toward women. Why? Simple: As these studies point out, in modern culture, women are the gatekeepers in marriage. As Dr. Laura says in *The Proper Care and Feeding of Husbands*, "Because the truth is that when it comes to home and relationships, women rule".[4]

Wives might be shocked to hear this, but a husband will live to make his wife happy. I am not saying he does or even knows how, only that making his wife happy is the number one goal for almost every man when he is happy himself. This does not mean there is nothing

---

[3] "Who initiates the divorce more often, the wife or the husband?" Divorce-lawyer-source.com, Accessed March 8, 2016, http://www.divorce-lawyer-source.com/faq/emotional/who-initiates-divorce-men-or-women.html

[4] Schlessinger, Dr. Laura (2009). *The Proper Care and Feeding of Husbands* New York: Harper Perennial, p. 64.

the husband can do. Men, your wife wants your love more than anything in the world, and when you learn to love her the way she needs to be loved, both of you will be transformed.

'Til Death Do Us Part?

On February 13, 2012, *The Washington Post* published an article entitled "Five myths about cheating."[5] In it, author Eric Anderson reported a shocking research study by renowned sex researcher Shere Hite, who discovered that seventy percent of married women cheat on their husbands. In a follow-up study, she found that seventy-two percent of married men cheat on their wives. Those who lack the fortitude for divorce sometimes turn to pornography, which is just another form of unfaithfulness.

What is happening in marriage today that has led to such shocking rates of divorce and infidelity? There are reasons, but few people are talking about them. These are what I call the enigmas in the marriage bedroom. Once we understand these invisible forces, we will be able to take corrective action.

Do not make the mistake of assuming this cannot happen to your marriage. In *His Needs, Her Needs: Building An Affair-Proof Marriage*, Willard F. Harley, Jr.

---

[5] Eric Anderson (February 13, 2012), "Five myths about cheating," *Washington Post,* accessed January 20, 2016, https://www.washingtonpost.com/opinions/five-myths-about-cheating/2012/02/08/gIQANGdaBR_story.html

reported that even strong religious and moral convictions do not stop people when it comes to affairs. Every couple is susceptible to the possibility of one person having an affair. The seventy percent of women and seventy-two percent of men would have undoubtedly denied that unfaithfulness could happen in their marriage. Most people do not enter marriage with designs of infidelity.

Marriages today also have to contend with more than simple affairs. Now "players" (men and women) have learned the science of seduction. These people make a game of seducing spouses with little regard for the sanctity of marriage. This has become a thousand times worse, as there are books, websites, and even classes devoted to teaching men how to seduce another man's wife. Many men have discovered it is far easier to seduce a married woman than a single woman. Although this may seem upside down, I will explain how this happens in a later chapter. This is far more common than you might think. Unfortunately, most people, especially in the Church, have not been educated about this phenomenon.

I say all of this to point out marriage is under attack like never before. Our culture tells us we can be happy without getting married, that marriages don't last, that marriage is no boundary to extra-curricular affairs, and that married people end up hating each other. Contrary to this opinion, I believe you can have a marriage filled with intimacy, joy, and happiness. But you must be willing to do the work required to keep these emotions alive or bring them back to life in your marriage. No matter how desperate your situation, there is no need to accept that you are doomed to a mediocre marriage with no solutions. But first, we must examine the facts about what really happens in marriage.

2

WHERE IN TARNATION IS THE MARRIAGE MANUAL?

How would you like to climb into the cockpit of a two-engine jet aircraft and attempt to fly it without proper training? Probably not, and yet that is about the equivalent of what we do when we get married. Your spouse is just as complicated as that aircraft, if not more so, but he or she did not come with a manual or an instructor. There is no marriage simulator in which we can practice either. (Although some people falsely believe they can take a trial run by living together first.) For many people, marriage is the most important decision they will ever make. Even so, we do not educate ourselves before climbing into the cockpit for our maiden flight. Left to our own devices, we tend to crash and burn repeatedly as we learn along life's way. These crashes can cause severe damage to the marriage relationship and to the individuals involved. Most of the damage can be repaired, but it takes time and effort.

Why is this? Where were our parents? Surely they must have known some of these difficult issues we all face in marriage. Did they just drop the ball and not pass the information on? Unfortunately, many of them simply stuck it out regardless of the state of their marriage, because there was a much greater stigma attached to divorce. The few couples who did have a great marriage had no idea why their marriage was different, so they were of no help either. Few people even knew what marriage was supposed to be, never mind how it worked.

What Is Marriage?

Marriage has been viewed differently throughout history, and it still varies a great deal from culture to culture. For most of history, however, marriage has had little to do with love. As Stephanie Coontz points out in her book *Marriage, A History: How Love Conquered Marriage,* love did not become a common reason for marriage until the late eighteenth century, and even then mostly in Western civilization. This is not to say that no one ever fell in love. People certainly hoped to love their spouse, but love as a reason for marriage was the exception. Parents arranged marriages, and most children had little influence on the selection of a spouse. Nevertheless, each partner had marital responsibilities that he or she took seriously, and people did what their partners, family, and society expected.

> Because marriage was too important a contract to be left up to the two individuals involved, kin, neighbors, and other outsiders, such as judges, priests, or government officials, were usually involved in negotiating a match. Even when individuals orchestrated their own transitions in and out of marriage, they frequently did so for

economic and political advantage rather than for love.

But only in the seventeenth century did a series of political, economic, and cultural changes in Europe begin to erode the older functions of marriage, encouraging individuals to choose their mates on the basis of personal affection and allowing couples to challenge the right of outsiders to intrude upon their lives. And not until the late eighteenth century, and then only in Western Europe and North America, did the notion of free choice and marriage for love triumph as a cultural ideal. [6]

In fact, the idea of marrying for love is so new in the history of the world that few have examined how love has changed marriage. When we marry for love, new problems enter marriages that were of little concern throughout most of history. For example, what happens if we stop loving our spouse or our spouse stops loving us? If we married for love, why stay married if we are no longer in love? "Tradition, tradition!" we hear, but what is traditional marriage? In biblical times, polygamy was common if the man could afford to purchase more than one wife. Bedding a servant (slave) was common as well. Think of Abraham and Hagar, for example. In Old

---

[6] Coontz, Stephanie (2006). *Marriage, a History: How Love Conquered Marriage*. New York: Penguin Publishing Group, p. 7.

Testament times, women were considered nothing more than property.

Marriage continues to evolve today, and the ground rules are changing constantly. This makes it difficult for many couples to catch their collective breath and resolve problems together. As noted above, the primary change has to do with the role love plays in marriage and also the changes in culture over the past several decades.

Since World War 2, for example, there has been a growing trend towards financial and societal independence for women. Before these changes occurred, women found it difficult to leave their husbands for both moral and financial reasons. Today, the stigma of being divorced has all but vanished, and financially, women are far more independent. Since this trend began, the rules of marriage have been in a constant state of flux. More recently, the definition of marriage is in flux as well. We can't even agree on a common definition of what marriage is. What are the expectations? What makes a good, happy, solid, intimate marriage? As a result, many couples are bailing out rather than sticking it out. Because of these changes, we need a new marriage manual to help us understand and navigate the new rules for having a blissful marriage. That's exactly what this book aspires to be.

It's Not Your Dream Job

Imagine a job where you get paid a million dollars a year. On top of that, you love doing the job and discover there are great fringe benefits. Astoundingly, you also find you only have to work a few hours each week. And, once at work, you discover everyone there loves you.

Does this sound possible to you? Does such a job even exist? Of course not! Yet, a great number of people enter marriage expecting exactly this sort of situation. Therefore, they are both unprepared and unwilling to take the time and effort required to have an intimate and healthy marriage. Most people believe the only key to a happy marriage is marrying the right person. Even so, people often enter marriage saying they understand a good marriage takes work, but then they refuse to do the heavy lifting needed. This is akin to thinking the dream job described above exists and refusing to accept anything less. Some people actually do less for their spouse after marriage. They act as though they have achieved their goal, and now they can relax.

Let me start by making one thing perfectly clear: If you want a dream spouse, you must be willing to become one yourself! That's going to take the right knowledge and a willingness to do what is needed. You might be wondering if you need to change first. The answer is *yes!* You are the one who must learn how to resolve the problems your marriage faces. If you and your spouse are reading this together, results will come much faster for both of you.

Marriage is not effortless. It requires attention, planning, thoughtful consideration, work, and sacrifice. If you are not willing to work hard to make your spouse happy, you have no business being married! That being said, the rewards for loving your spouse and meeting his or her needs are astounding.

Get to Know Your Co-pilot

Men spend a great deal of time trying to understand women, with little or no success, and women have the same trouble understanding men. Most women are clueless about men, yet just about all of them believe they understand men! In the same way, I have known many men who had little understanding of what they were feeling or why. Precious few women understand themselves either and why they feel certain emotions. You might be asking: What did I get myself into? Am I in over my head? I love my partner so deeply and want this marriage to work so we can be happy, but nothing seems to make it better!

Marriage does not have to be confusing, daunting, or frustrating. You can have a marriage that brings you and your partner great joy. This requires you to make the effort to understand your partner and do what is needed to meet his or her needs. There will be sacrifice, but the rewards are more than worth it.

In a later chapter I will set forth a set of common beliefs and commitments that I believe are necessary for all marriages if couples hope to achieve true love, intimacy, and happiness together. Obviously, couples with differing views about marriage will have greater conflicts. Ministers often give prospective partners tests to identify these differences. Hopefully, spouses will realize in advance the importance of these differences with their partner. The idea is to enlighten couples about potential difficulties.

My wife and I took such a test, and the results showed we are a great match. We were excited, because it showed we had made a wise partner selection. Yet, compatibility is not a guarantee of happiness. The important issues are the differences. Some people falsely believe differences make a marriage more exciting or more interesting. The truth is that more differences cause more problems. That being said, *all couples will experience differences and problems in marriage.* Yet, with a strong foundation built on the core set of principles and actions set forth in this book, I believe every marital problem can be dealt with and resolved in a loving manner.

Expectations: False or Real?

Girls grow up dreaming of the "big day." Many daydream of falling madly in love. Different dresses, different settings, but they all imagine themselves in a beautiful gown walking down the aisle to their Prince Charming. They play house as little girls and love to dress up in fancy dresses. It is their lifelong dream to grow up, fall in love, and be loved by the perfect man. They dream about getting married and having children together. They want to be deeply in love and be deeply loved by Prince Charming and live happily ever after. Little girls do this repeatedly. Are you picking up on the point about females here?

Boys, on the other hand, do not give much thought to marriage before they enter puberty. After all, until boys reach puberty, most girls have "cooties." That said, a boy of any age can be captivated by a pretty girl. Although they have no idea why, even little boys are fascinated by the beauty of the female anatomy! In first grade I was spellbound by the beauty of my teacher and believed I would marry her when I grew up. The point is: visual interest in female beauty is in a man's DNA.

When males hit puberty and start to dream about marriage, they are far more likely to daydream about how beautiful she will be and making love with his wife. Then he dreams about how beautiful she will be and making love with his wife. Let's not forget, how beautiful she will be and how great it will be to make love with his wife as much as he wants, and then being loved by her and having children. Are you picking up on the point about males here?

As we grow up, reality begins to sink in. Women realize they are not going to marry a real prince. Men realize that the only place to find the perfect "ten" is in the movies or the airbrushed pages of a magazine or a photo-shopped picture online. Both males and females begin to embrace reality, at least to a degree. Both still harbor their primary dream, her prince and his princess.

Can couples realize this dream? Is it possible to have a fairytale marriage? This may surprise you, but I believe it is. How do I know? I'm in one right now. Is it perfect with no problems? No, not perfect, but absolutely wonderful! I want this for you, but it is going to take education, work, devotion, sacrifice, and commitment.

Love, Sweet Love

Most couples have a wonderful time during courtship. They feel close to each other. She usually dresses well, and he is a super gentleman. The more time they spend together, the deeper their feelings for each other grow until they love each other. She feels he is her prince, and he thinks she is his princess. The compliments roll off their tongues as they express appreciation for each other. He knows how to listen to her and comfort her, hold her, and be gentle and caring towards her. These things occur almost without effort, and in time, she begins to feel secure in his love. She is loving, and caring; her depth of understanding may feel like magic to him. She praises him regularly, and he feels good whenever she is around. Once again, it seems like she can make him feel loved and secure without much effort. Most people look back at their courtship with great fondness. How wonderful it was to fall in love with that special person!

She is doing new activities with him, perhaps even activities she would not enjoy normally, but because she is with him, she enjoys them. He is working hard to let her know how much he loves her. Eventually, they begin dreaming about being married to each other. They declare their love for each other, and when they hear how much the other person loves them, too, they are walking on air. Don't you wish that time could last forever?

Then he pops the question, and she says *yes*. They start looking forward to married life together and how wonderful it will be. Their love makes them feel like they can take on the world. She knows he has some quirks, but she can accept them, because he is so wonderful. He looks at her and dreams about how he will enjoy making love to her for the rest of his life.

During courtship, they feel the other person is so special and so wonderful, but how did this happen? Was it karma? Fate? Providence? Is there a way to keep this love alive forever?

Sweet Paula

I met my wife through E-harmony. I looked at her picture, read her profile several times, and then read over 250 questions she had answered about herself. There was so much information about her that I felt as though I knew her before I even contacted her. Not only was she what I was looking for in a woman, she described me almost perfectly when defining her ideal man.

She was so right for me that I began to love her even before I met her. In fact, I turned to a friend who was sitting with me and said, "I'm going to marry this one right here!" even though Paula and I had not exchanged a single word of correspondence. My friend thought I was crazy, but today, she is my beautiful bride, and we are deeply in love.

Did this happen by accident? Was I just lucky? No. Am I blessed by God? You better believe it! I thank God for Paula every day, but it took action on my part to make it happen. There's a song by Dolly Parton and Kenny Rogers called "Islands in the Stream." The song starts with Kenny singing the following words, "Baby, when I met you there was peace unknown, I set out to get you with a fine-toothed comb." In the same way, I determined to make Paula fall in love with me, and she did.

You might be wondering: Can you make someone fall in love with you? Did I make this sweet, beautiful inside and out, woman fall in love with me? The great news is, yes I did, using a method for love I developed after studying this subject in great depth and then putting what I learned into action.

Does Paula feel like she was tricked or deceived into loving me? No, Paula says she is thrilled to have me for her husband, and all those things I did to make her fall in love with me are precious memories for us both. Let me share how our romance began just to give you an idea.

After writing back and forth for some time, getting my Sweet Paula to meet with me was turning out to be a real challenge. She was in no hurry at all. What could I do? If I pushed too hard, I would come across as desperate. The last thing I wanted was for her to think of me as a stalker.

She had commented in her profile about a book she had read called *Love Does* by Bob Goff, which had touched her heart. I read the book, and then I used passages from it in the hope of touching her heart and getting her to meet with me. The book contained the author's love story and how he had won his "Sweet Marie." So I asked Paula how I would ever find out if she was my "Sweet Paula" if she didn't meet with me. I suspect she chuckled at that, but it did not move her.

Then I read a chapter in Goff's book called "Just Say Yes." It tells the story of how God made a big change in the author's life because he had "just said yes" to one special meeting. Because he said yes, God was able to move in a spectacular way. So I told my Sweet Paula that Bob would tell her to "just say yes" to meeting me. That was enough to touch her heart and get her thinking it could be true, so she finally agreed to meet.

When the big day arrived, I went to a florist and picked out a huge Gerber daisy to give her. Arriving at the restaurant early, I met with the hostess, reserved an out-of-the-way booth, and had the flower waiting on the table for her.

Our first meeting was a huge success as we laughed and even cried together. That was just the beginning. I romanced this woman's socks off! Later, she told me the flower I selected was wonderful, just right. She told her friends and family, "This man is sweeping me off my feet. He is very special, the real deal."

At our wedding reception, we played a video interview of the two of us talking about how I had courted her and how we had fallen so deeply in love. The rest of our story is more romantic than I explained.

Later, after seeing the interview and learning the actions I had taken to make her fall in love with me, her cousin came up to me and said, "You have a real passion for Paula." He was right, and that passion is as strong today as it was the day we got married.

My point is, love is not an accident over which you have no control. There are specific actions you take that will cause your partner to fall in love with you and then love you more and more. It is within your control. You can cause your partner to love you or hate you depending how you treat him or her. This book is designed to teach you how to get your partner to love you more deeply. I'm not talking about gimmicks or tricks but rather understanding your spouse and then meeting his or her special needs and desires in a way that makes him or her adore you. Do you want that? Are you willing to work for it? Then read on.

3

THE DOWNWARD SPIRAL IN MARRIAGE

After a couple gets married, regular life begins. He returns to work, and in most cases, she does, too. For a while, things seem pretty good, even wonderful as they soar through life together at a high altitude with great intimacy. In time though, they find things are slowing down. He is not nearly as romantic, and she has also cooled off a great deal in her sexual desire for him. Their engines (hearts) are receiving less fuel (love) from each other, and the relationship begins to lose altitude as intimacy declines. Both spouses agree this is normal and is just a part of life. They surmise that no one honeymoons every day of the year. They are right, but they are also wrong. Although this is common in marriage, loss of intimacy does not have to happen! Unfortunately, this is just the beginning.

Things are changing, and neither spouse understands why. Her sexual desire for him continues to diminish, and his affection and quality time with her decreases. He may no longer listen well to her concerns. He also becomes increasingly frustrated with her, perhaps a bit withdrawn as well, and she doesn't understand why. As a result, both start to feel loved a little less. Regular reductions in love are being made in each other's hearts, and the two do not realize the seriousness of what has started to happen to their beautiful love for each other.

They have begun what I call the downward spiral in marriage. She realizes she does not have near the sex drive he continues to have. He realizes he can have hugs anytime, but they mean little to him, as they rarely lead anywhere, so they lose the comfort they used to give. She begins to withdraw from lovemaking, slowly at first, but over time, it becomes a major slowdown. He is no longer giving her much quality time and affection either. In fact, sometimes she may think he's a real jerk! At times, he may seem callous or uncaring. Regular love reductions are being made in both hearts with few increases, and no one understands why or how to stop it.

Then the situation peaks. An argument or strong disagreement ensues over an unrelated issue. After making up, they engage in "makeup sex," and their relationship soars. They have a romantic time, and all seems right with their marriage again, but their relationship does not return to its original level, and another downward spiral begins.

During downward spirals, men find themselves feeling bitter towards their wife. These feelings show themselves through various behaviors that make significant love reductions, causing their partner's heart to sputter or stall and the relationship to lose altitude. Unfortunately, this cycle tends to repeat itself, each time beginning from a lower altitude. Significant reductions in love are being made, followed by a few increases, and each spouse can feel it in his or her heart.

For a while, most couples assume they are going through the normal adjustment of familiarity. Friends may tell them the honeymoon is over. Most marriage counselors believe the couples' original feelings of romance are bound to decrease. They say the original depth of feelings is temporary, because they are based on fantasy rather than reality. Those feelings necessarily diminish to more sensible levels once regular life takes over. I could not disagree more! That seemingly magical feeling you felt so deeply from and for your spouse can be restored permanently.

To fully understand how that can happen—and what causes the downward spiral in the first place—we need to learn more about how the heart gives and receives love.

How Love Works

Many couples reminisce about their courting days and how magical everything seemed. They fell in love, and it was wonderful. Some believe that love was just a chance meeting with the right person. Others believe falling in love was destiny. Still others credit God, karma, or "chemistry." Regardless of what you believe, your spouse loves you because of the way you make your spouse feel! How deeply your spouse loves you is a direct result of how you treat him or her.

Although I have read about this in more than one book, I have to give credit to Willard F. Harley, Jr. for being the first to outline a process by which people fall in and out of love. In his book *His Needs, Her Needs, Building An*

Affair-Proof Marriage, he describes what he calls the "love bank," wherein people make deposits or withdrawals from each other's accounts. Although not perfect, his analogy shows how people can fall in and out of love with someone. When someone makes deposits in our love bank, our feelings toward them grow. When that person makes withdrawals, our love for him or her diminishes.

I have understood these basic principles for some time, but Harley helped me to appreciate them in greater depth. Still, something didn't feel quite right about it. I could see how using his love bank principle worked, but in the end, it did not jell completely. Finally, it hit me why his analogy seemed to be off, so I came up with what I believe to be a much more accurate way to describe why we love each other and the way intimacy occurs. I realized I could turn the art of love into a "science" that everyone could understand and apply. Once we understand that we can make someone love or stop loving us with our actions and that it is easy to do, we can control our love destiny. Harley wrote the best book on marriage I have ever read, and I am certain he has helped a great deal of people, but I would like to move the ball further down the court, so to speak, by increasing our understanding of marriage and intimacy.

The Love Throttle

Like an aircraft, every person has what I call a "love throttle" for each relationship in his or her life that can increase or decrease depending on how they are treated. How much we care for someone depends on the position of our love throttle. If we have a great love for someone, the throttle is pushed forward. When we feel overwhelming love for a person, the throttle goes beyond 100 percent and can move all the way to 110 percent, just like in a real aircraft. This maximum position is usually reserved for our spouse when we are feeling immense intimacy with him or her. The key point to remember is that you do not control your love throttle. That role belongs to your spouse.

A real aircraft also has thrust reverse to slow the aircraft down when landing or taxiing. In the same way, when we find ourselves disliking or feeling disdain for someone, our thrust reversers are engaged, and our love throttle increases reverse power. The more we dislike the person, the higher the reverse power. Also, just like a real aircraft, engaging your partner's thrust reverser while in midair can tear your marriage apart or, at minimum, do severe damage to your relationship.[7] Sometimes this damage can be repaired, but it requires significant time and sacrifice.

As stated earlier, a marriage relationship has two engines (hearts) like a twin-engine aircraft, the husband's and the wife's. For the relationship to fly to a high altitude (deep intimacy), both engines must be running at top speed.

Love throttles are moved forward by "love actions." (I will define eleven distinct love actions later in this book.) It takes all of them being done well regularly,

---

[7] "Lauda Air Flight 004." Wikpedia.org, accessed March 8, 2016, https://en.wikipedia.org/wiki/Lauda_Air_Flight_004

plus placing your spouse above everyone and everything else in your life (except God), to push your partner's love throttle to one hundred percent or beyond. When you reach this point with your partner, you will find you have amazing intimacy together.

Earlier, I said that I swept my Sweet Paula off her feet and that she fell in love with me. It all began with understanding that everyone has a love throttle. Then I applied my love actions method and my understanding of how to move her love throttle forward, which I will discuss later. You need to know more than how the love throttle works though. You need to make significant increases and few decreases in your spouse's throttle position. This means you need a good understanding of the opposite sex and your spouse's specific needs and desires. Although some people have some understanding of the opposite sex, most people have a hard time understanding the way their other half thinks. So many times I have heard people say, "I just don't understand her," or "What was he thinking?" This is the *Men are from Mars and Women are from Venous* scenario. We will cover those differences in this book as well. In the meantime, here is a scenario to give you an idea of how the love throttle concept works.

Tim & Debbie: Making Increases and Decreases in Love Throttle Position

When Tim met Debbie, he thought she was beautiful. Her hair was gorgeous, she was just the right

---

46

height, her clothes were feminine, and she had a certain elegance about her. Just because Tim was so attracted to her and because she seemed almost perfect to him, she received two nudges forward on Tim's love throttle. When Tim inquired about Debbie to learn more, he discovered she was single, involved in her church, and loved children. Debbie received another love throttle increase for being the kind of woman Tim was seeking.

Tim asked Debbie out on a date, but Debbie was unsure of Tim. She didn't know much about him, so she told Tim she didn't know him well enough to date him. Tim was disappointed, and this took away one of the increases on Tim's love throttle position Debbie had achieved without any effort on her part. Still, Tim thought, *I want to date her.*

As time went on, Debbie got to know Tim better. Tim would flirt with her and compliment her. Soon, she began to trust Tim more and to feel comfortable around him. Tim made every effort to help Debbie feel at ease, which caused three increases in Debbie's love throttle. Finally, Debbie agreed to go on a date with Tim. This made him feel wonderful. Debbie got back that lost increase and added two more nudges to Tim's love throttle.

They went out to dinner and had a wonderful time together. The conversation flowed with ease. Tim told Debbie he thought she was beautiful and intelligent, a rare combination. As Debbie got to know Tim better, she found him to be a kind and considerate man. By the end of the date, both had accrued four more increases. Tim had nudged seven increases on Debbie's love throttle, and Debbie had nine on Tim's.

Tim called Debbie and asked her if she would be interested in going to a concert with him the following Friday. Debbie said that she had already made plans with her mother, but she would love to have a rain check. Tim was disappointed. Even though Debbie had offered him a rain check, he could not help but feel let down. Debbie lost one notch from Tim's love throttle through no fault of her own.

Tim was surprised the next day when Debbie called and suggested they go to the county fair together. He soared with happiness. Not only did Debbie regain her lost increase, such an effort showed that Debbie must care for him, so she gained two more increases. Debbie had moved Tim's love throttle forward eleven times.

Over the next few weeks, Tim and Debbie started doing more things together. Debbie saw that Tim was punctual, honest, and hardworking, someone who cared about how she felt. He had a romantic side as well. These things caused significant increases in Debbie's love throttle. Tim saw that Debbie was a caring, thoughtful, and affectionate woman. His hugs and touches were always welcomed, so Debbie also made significant increases in Tim's love throttle. Both were making substantial, regular increases in each other's love throttle. At the end of three months of dating, Tim had caused 312 increases, and Debbie had caused 335. Each felt the other was special, and both began to think this might be "the one."

Whenever something was bothering Debbie, Tim listened patiently as Debbie shared her feelings. This took little effort on Tim's part, because he was genuinely concerned about her. Debbie found she could call Tim after work each day, and when she shared her day with him, he loved hearing about it. When Tim shared about his aspirations for his career, Debbie listened carefully. Then she told Tim she was impressed with how much he had accomplished in such a short time and that she was certain he would achieve his goals. Tim loved that Debbie expressed confidence in his abilities and his intelligence. Both Tim and Debbie, almost without effort, continued to make significant increases in each other's love throttle positon.

One evening while out on a date Tim found he couldn't contain himself anymore, and he confessed to Debbie how deeply he was falling in love with her. Debbie told Tim that she loved him, too, and they embraced in a wonderful kiss that felt like magic. Now that they had both said, "I love you," thoughts began to surface about their future together.

After about six months of blissful dating, both had accrued well over eight hundred increases in each other's love throttle, and now they were thinking about wedding bells. Tim believed Debbie had sent the signals that should he ask her to marry him, she would most likely agree. This signal caused a major increase in Tim's love throttle position, and Tim began to think he could not imagine a future without Debbie. He sent the signal that he was thinking about marrying Debbie, and that made a major increase in her love throttle position as well.

Finally, Tim planned a wonderful date together. Towards the end of the date, Tim got down on one knee, opened a small box with a diamond ring inside, and confessed the depth of his love. He said he did not want to live without her by his side, and he asked Debbie to be his wife. Tears of joy streamed down Debbie's face as she said how deeply she loved him, too. Debbie found herself saying, "Yes, yes, yes!" They embraced in a huge, almost magical kiss as they made more significant increases in each other's love throttle position. Their engines were running strong, and the two gained altitude together. Both had love throttle increases of more than one thousand, and the relationship felt like a fairytale to them. Both began daydreaming about being married.

Unfortunately, planning the wedding was not nearly as easy as Tim and Debbie thought, especially once they had to consider other family members and their wishes. Although Tim had agreed to get married in Debbie's church, Tim's parents were upset about that. Tim also believed Debbie's mother was doing more to plan the wedding than Debbie and that Debbie was letting her mother railroad her. As Tim and Debbie discussed these difficult issues and defended their parents, their love throttles slipped back a few notches. Tim and Debbie found themselves in their first real disagreement, and it took a toll on them. They wished there was a way to please their parents and each other.

Both sets of parents began to see the difficulty they were causing and tried to compromise. Finally, Tim and Debbie made their own decision and notified their parents of their verdict. They had weathered their first real disagreement, and although they solved it together, each had caused the other's love throttle to slip back. Now they were both running at about 850.

As the problems receded behind them, they began to find joy in each other once again, and then they started planning their honeymoon together. This went smoothly, and once again, each of their love throttles surged forward. By the time they reached their wedding day, they had recovered all the lost momentum, and with all the additional increases, each was running now at a whopping twelve hundred.

After the wedding, Tim and Debbie had a wonderful honeymoon together. They made love often, and they felt closer to each other than ever. Now that they were husband and wife, they were happy and continued to make regular increases to each other's love throttle. By the end of the honeymoon, Debbie was at 1320, and Tim was at 1330.

For the next six months, increases and decreases occurred in each of their love throttles, but at the end of that time, both Tim and Debbie were at 1400. Married life was great, and both believed it would be that way forever. Unfortunately, this was their all-time high, because their love would never be that high again. Things could have continued to increase a great deal if Tim and Debbie understood how to love each other. Unfortunately, neither understood how to control each other's love throttles, so they were unprepared for the deceleration that was about to occur.

I understand you are probably anxious to dig right into the enigmas. However, to understand what they are and how they interact, it is important to understand not only the "love throttle" concept but also the "love actions" that make it move. Love actions increase the love we feel towards someone by fueling our heart and moving our love throttle forward.

4

LOVE ACTIONS

Love actions are things we do for our partner that are especially important and make him or her feel loved. The degree of influence these love actions have is different for each person, and there is an even greater difference between women and men. When you fell in love, you and your partner were doing a good job at making regular increases by doing some of these things, probably without even realizing it.

Some authors have discovered this and articulated beliefs about some of these actions. I spoke earlier of a method for making someone fall in love. The love actions listed here are that method. When understood and implemented, they can push your partner's love throttle so far forward they overflow with love for you. Failing to do these actions will cause automatic decreases!

In *His Needs, Her Needs*, Willard F. Harley, Jr. says the number one need for a woman is affection, and the number one need for a man is sex. If a woman isn't getting affection from him and he isn't getting sex from her, neither partner will feel loved, and they will have problems in their marriage, which leaves both susceptible to an affair. Harley also points out the need to do recreational things together and the need for quality time in every marriage. Each time we do these things with/for our partner, we make deposits in their love bank. Each time we do negative things, we make withdrawals.

Similarly, in *The Five Love Languages*, Gary Chapman argues that there are five love languages. These are: Touch, Words of Affirmation, Acts of Service, Gifts, and Quality Time. According to Chapman, these should be put in order of priority by each spouse so the other will understand what is important and meet his or her partner's needs. He uses the term "love tank," but the principle is the same as the love bank. His book has helped many couples learn how to love each other better.

Both authors are correct, yet neither goes nearly far enough, because neither identifies the marriage enigmas or the downward spiral that occurs in almost every marriage. Plus, a great deal more needs to be explained about the male and female sex drive, both of which are misunderstood by both men and women.

To help illuminate these facts, here are the eleven love actions that I believe are critical to moving your partner's love throttle forward. Every couple needs these eleven actions to occur regularly if they hope to have a happy, intimate marriage. If any love actions are missing, the couple may not weather or recover from the downward spiral that happens to almost every couple. After reading this, you will understand why merely applying the throttle is not enough if your relationship is in a downward spiral. You need to move your partner's love throttle in the right way and at the right time in order to pull your marriage out of a dive and regain altitude.

1. Affection

The Oxford dictionary defines affection as "a gentle feeling of fondness or liking." Affection is the act of providing an attitude of love and gentleness in the way we convey ourselves to our spouse. *Affection sets the tone for all communication, both verbal and physical, between spouses.* If a couple does not deal with each other affectionately, communication will not be effective. Controlling your emotions and making certain you deal gently and affectionately with your spouse will cause major love throttle increases. Dealing with your partner in a harsh manner will lead to major decreases.

Although husbands enjoy affection as well, it is of primary importance to women. In fact, *affection is a woman's primary love action need.* All interactions between couples need to occur within this loving and gentle atmosphere. A wife will feel secure when she knows her husband is always going to deal with her in an attitude of love and kindness. Providing steady affection to your wife will make huge increases in her love throttle. Your wife will feel secure that she can trust that you will honor her need to live in an atmosphere of love. Affection is critical for the marriage to have happiness and intimacy.

2. Quality Time

Quality time is time spent together without distractions or interruptions. It is time when your attention is focused solely on your spouse. Quality time says, "You are important to me!" Although some people think women need this more than men, in truth, it is just as important for each partner, just in different ways. No marriage relationship should have less than fourteen hours of quality time each week. That's the equivalent of two hours a day. In *His Needs, Her Needs,* Harley says no less than fifteen hours. I chose fourteen hours, because it is easier to divide into the equivalent of two hours each day. The truth is, the amount of time you and your partner need may be different from others. But if you do err, make certain the error is more than enough quality time together. Fourteen hours is about eight percent of each day devoted to one-on-one time with the most important person in your life. Different activities can and will occur during quality time that are essential to marital growth and happiness. Quality time proves the importance of the relationship and makes large increases in your partner's love throttle, resulting in more love flowing back to you as well.

3. Respect

The Oxford dictionary defines respect as "a deep feeling of admiration for someone or something elicited by their abilities, qualities, or achievements." This action is of utmost importance for men. A husband's need for respect cannot be over-stated. A wife who shows respect towards her husband regularly will make major increases in his love throttle. In the same way, a disrespectful wife is devastating to a husband's happiness and self-esteem and makes colossal decreases to his love throttle.

This is of such importance and magnitude that entire books and book chapters have been written about the importance of wives respecting their husbands. In *For Her Only*, Shaunte Feldhahn reports that many men would rather be respected, than loved by their wife.[8] Think about the magnitude of this statement. Dr. Emerson Eccerichs wrote half a book about the importance of respect for the man called *Love and Respect: The Love She Most Desires and The Respect He Desperately Needs*. If a wife does not show great respect for her husband, she will never have a happy or intimate marriage. Although a wife might gain a great short-term victory over her husband by belittling him, this causes huge decreases in his love throttle and comes at a great long-term cost. She may not realize the magnitude of her actions or understand they are self-defeating until it's too late. Although this is a primary love need for men, women need to feel respected too, so let your wife know how proud you are of her as often as possible.

---

[8] Feldhahn, Shaunti (2008). *For Women Only, Revised and Updated Edition: What You Need to Know about the Inner Lives of Men.* Sisters, OR: Multnomah Books, p. 15–16

4. Sharing Emotions

This is another primary love action required by women. Women have an inherent need to express their emotions through conversation. This may be as simple as asking how her day went or going deep on a particular issue. Either way, she needs her husband to listen and acknowledge how she is feeling about what she is conveying. Husbands should not offer suggestions, try to help, or fix their wife's issues in any way during this time unless she asks for his help. It is not necessarily about the problem; it is about her sharing how she feels about the problem and him listening. This may come as a surprise to men, but it is essential to your wife's happiness that you simply listen to her when she expresses herself in conversation. When you listen attentively to her concerns, she will feel that you care about her and her feelings. This behavior will make huge love throttle increases in your wife as she sees you care genuinely about her feelings.

Men, there may be times when the things she wants to get off her mind are about you. It may be difficult to listen when you are the subject of her complaint, but try to remain silent unless she asks something of you.

The 70/30 rule applies here as well. Sometimes men need to express themselves without their wives trying to fix their problems or resolve their issue. Talking and listening should be part of quality time, and there needs to be time for the husband to express his feelings about things he deems important to discuss as well.

5. Hugs, Kisses, and Holding

Hugs, kisses, and holding are primarily love actions that husbands do for their wife, and they should occur regularly. If the only time you touch your wife is to request sex, she will begin to feel like a sexual object and withdraw physically. Men need to realize that women do not feel love through sex (more on that later) and make certain they show their wives a good deal of physical contact apart from sex.

Watch your wife. She hugs relatives, friends, children, puppies, even stuffed animals. Most women cannot be hugged too much. You may find yourself winding up sexually every time you come near your wife, which is fine, but you need to keep it to yourself. This is also important after your wife has given herself to you in lovemaking. Take time to hold, hug, and appreciate her. After sex you may be feeling loved, but your wife may not, and taking time for her afterwards goes a long way toward her not feeling like a sexual object. You might think this should fall under the "Act of Touch" section, but the need for touch in order to feel loved has nothing to do with this. Others may feel that this is part of affection, but remember, for the purposes of this book, affection is to be *the continual attitude* for all communication, both verbal and physical. Hugs, kisses, and holding are physical acts apart from sex done affectionately to convey love to your partner and make huge love throttle increases.

6. Sex

This is the primary love action men need to receive. It is through the act of sex that a husband receives the strongest and most important feelings of love from his wife. Most women think of sex as a physical act and fail to understand that for their husband, it is far more. Sex is essential to a husband's happiness, self-esteem and overall sense of well-being. Without regular sex, a husband will not feel loved by his wife. This also ties into the respect and quality time I spoke of earlier. There is so much information to learn about sex that I have devoted entire sections of this book to it. The male sex drive is one of the enigmas in marriage we will discuss shortly. This love action has the potential to make major increases or decreases in a husband's love throttle.

7. Acts of Service

This is an area in which many people err. They work hard to do things for their spouse but receive little appreciation for their efforts, which causes love throttle decreases. Just because an act of service means a great deal to you does not mean your spouse assigns the same value to it as you do.

It is important to talk with your spouse during quality time and discover which acts of service are important. Your actions could be of little value if you do not learn what is important to your spouse. Once you know which acts of service are important to your spouse, make certain you do some or all of them regularly. This takes work, but this action also makes big love throttle increases. Finally, acts of service are just as important to men as to women.

8. Words of Praise

You should speak words of praise to and about your spouse every day. This makes huge love throttle increases. If you can't find wonderful things to say about your spouse, you have a serious problem. Here are a few examples for you: "I am so in love with you. You are the love of my life. You are so wonderful. You have always been special to me. I am amazed how beautiful you are even when you wake up in the morning. You are so incredibly intelligent. You are the kindest person I have ever known. You are the best person I have ever known. I am so proud you are my husband. My wife is the best. I am so grateful for the husband God has given me. I am blessed to be married to you."

Get the idea? The list is endless, and your spouse needs to know you are grateful to be married to him or her. Huge increases in their love throttle!

9. Gifts

Everyone enjoys receiving gifts, especially the right gifts. Some people appreciate gifts more than others. Your spouse may appreciate gifts a great deal or just a little. Gifts are a way to say "I love you" to your spouse. Gifts also let your spouse know you are thinking of him or her when your spouse is not present. If your spouse appreciates gifts, give them often. It never hurts to make extra increases in your partner's love throttle. Don't wait until you need to say, "I'm sorry," to give a gift. They should be a regular part of your relationship.

Men, if your wife enjoys cards or flowers, don't wait for some special occasion or until you've done something wrong. Slip a card into her purse that she will find while she is at work. Send her flowers when she least expects them. Be creative and romantic! Just showing you adore her will nudge her throttle forward.

Gifts are not always objects either. A wife can make a romantic candlelight dinner, put on some sexy lingerie, and then make passionate love with her husband. I can't imagine any man not appreciating that gift!

10. Touch

Everyone needs a certain amount of touch. Your spouse may need a good deal of touch to feel loved by you. Touch should not be confused with affection or sex. Although touch is a form of affection and sex is a form of touch, for the purposes of this book, they're separate. Plus, the way you touch your spouse speaks volumes about how you feel about him or her. Touching your spouse in the right way will make significant increases in his or her love throttle position. Some types of touch include gently rubbing your spouse's back or feet, holding hands, walking arm-in-arm, and cuddling.

11. Recreational Time

Although I have always known how important this is to me personally, I have to give a hat tip to Harley for this one. This is an act of love primarily for men. Husbands need and want their wife to do recreational things with them. However, a husband's need for recreational time with his wife can become a serious point of contention in a marriage if she refuses to participate. Couples need to find recreational activities they enjoy doing together. A wife who does recreational things with her husband will make big increases in his love throttle.

A word of warning: Spending recreational time with someone of the opposite sex other than your spouse can easily lead to an affair, even in a good marriage. Ignore this warning at your peril!

Doing these love actions and making certain your partner's love throttle position is high at all times will help you increase the level of intimacy in your marriage and protect it against the problems or enigmas I am about to present.

5

THE FIRST ENIGMA

Most men, and some women, will find the information presented in this chapter upsetting. Try not to be discouraged. I promise I will not leave you hanging without solutions. Remember, the purpose of this book is to help you have a great marriage. We can't fix anything though if we don't take an honest look at the problems, and this first enigma is huge.

The Wife's Sexual Desire for Her Husband Diminishes

Many scholarly books have been written about females and their desire for sex. Yet, when it comes to marriage, we never read the plain truth, so here it is: After marriage, a wife's sexual desire for her husband diminishes. Over time, every married woman is going to discover that she does not have nearly the same sexual desire for her husband as she once had. How long this takes and how much it diminishes is different for every woman, but it will happen! If this decline in her sex drive is allowed to foster, the marriage can go from a downward spiral into a tailspin. Eventually, a wife may cease wanting any sex with her husband at all!

A wife's drive for her husband begins to fall just a few months, if not a few weeks, after being married and continues to diminish. When this begins, a couple's love throttles are generally sitting at an all-time high, so they are able to weather this quite well for a time. But eventually, the husband asks his wife what is going on. Usually, she is clueless. All she knows is she does not feel nearly the same desire for sex that she used to feel. Men tend to attribute this to a failing in themselves, and it can be devastating to the male ego.

At this point, many women end up in their doctor's office to see if anything is wrong with them. The doctor almost always reports the woman is fine. This leads to confusion. She does not understand why she is losing sexual desire for the man she loves. She may surmise that since nothing is wrong with her, the problem must be with him. Although a great number of women and men come to this conclusion, they are wrong. His behavior in response to her diminishing drive may have eased back her love throttle, but it is not the primary reason for her loss of desire. In fact, the situation is just the opposite from what most women assume.

Instead of causing her slowdown, her slowdown has devastated him emotionally, and he is reacting from a position of hurt and ignorance. He is at a loss and doesn't know what to do. The man may start questioning his masculinity, his attractiveness, his ability to please any woman, never mind his wife. Most men are so confused by what is happening that they do not know what to do or think. So they become angry and bitter as they are made to feel like a villain merely for desiring their own wife!

If the woman decides her lack of drive is due to her husband, she will usually try to get him to change the behaviors she believes are causing the problem. She may even have a list of things he does that irritate her. By that point, the husband is usually so desperate for his wife's sexual affections that he is willing to do almost anything to get her to make love to him more frequently again. Yet, even though he may bend over backwards to try and make her happy, nothing helps her regain her desire. In fact, it can have just the opposite effect if he gives in to her demands, because she may lose respect for him for letting her walk all over him. This is like applying more power while an airplane is in a nose dive. This action just hastens the crash. It can be a real catch-22 for the husband, as he is condemned to failure either way.

Some couples ignore the problem or suck it up and downplay the importance of sex in their marriage. They convince themselves that sex is not all there is to life. The wife usually convinces the husband to go along, thinking it is normal. Some couples may even report a happy marriage right up until they file for divorce. Clueless about how to resolve the problem, men pretend it is not an issue, because aside from little or no sex, they still love their wife.

Some women, influenced perhaps by their mothers or women of faith, spiral down to a certain point and begin doing what I call "maintenance lovemaking."

They do what they believe is the bare minimum necessary to keep their husband happy or what they believe they are morally obligated to do. Unfortunately, they are wrong. What they actually have is a husband who is hurt, broken, and ripe for an affair! Whether he admits it or even realizes it himself, a husband who is neglected in the bedroom can easily be seduced or fall in love with another woman!

What I have just described to you is universal. Every woman's desire for her husband will decrease after being married. This is our first enigma. A wife's sexual desire for her husband diminishes over time.

I began researching this by talking about it with every married woman I met. Unfortunately, most of the women I knew did not want to admit the truth. They would hem and haw at the question. But every married woman I spoke with who was not a regular acquaintance of mine spoke openly and reported the same thing. They either had lost or were losing sexual interest in their husband. Even the women who cut my hair (young women who had only been married a couple of years) reported being bored sexually with their husband. Some wished there was a way to spice things up. One of my wife's friends said she was not bored with her husband, just uninterested in sex with him. Regardless of how you frame it, the problem exists.

When I first discovered this, at first, I was relieved it wasn't just me. That was short-lived when I realized the end result was the same—no sex! It was so disturbing to me that I was upset about it for months. My entire dream of being married had just blown up in my face. No matter who my wife was, after a certain time, she would no longer desire me. Even if I were to divorce and remarry, the downward spiral would begin again.

Hurt and angry, I searched and prayed for answers. I read books and scoured the Internet. Surely I could not be alone in discovering this. But I was stunned at the lack of information. How was it possible that more people didn't know about something this profound? It seemed like every man—and woman—was blind to this enigma. How could this be?

Finally, I came across a book called *Women's Infidelity: Living in Limbo* by Michelle Langley. She had also discovered that a woman's sexual desire for their husband goes down immensely after marriage. She had conducted a survey of over 150 married women and written a book on the subject. She wrote from a secular liberal point of view and seemed to have a chip on her shoulder towards men, conveying a "they deserve it" attitude. Although her attitude towards men seemed heartless to me, that did not change what her research revealed.

Unfortunately, she offered no solutions. She had a "men are scum anyway" attitude, and this was simply payback time. For her, this discovery was liberating. She says she believes the decline in a wife's desire for her husband is because monogamy is not a natural state for women. She acts as though everything is merely biology. Morals and fidelity are merely disposable items. She hopes that revealing what happens to a married woman's sex drive will help married women feel that having multiple sex partners is normal and natural. In her mind, there is no problem to solve. All women need to do is understand that having great sex with a man other than their husband is normal and healthy.

The cold, hard fact is that a woman's desire for her husband diminishes over time. Please note that I did not say her sexual desire diminishes, just her sexual desire *for her husband*. Initially, she may believe her entire sex drive has diminished; but this is dangerous thinking, because it leaves her wide open to seduction and an affair.

Now, I know what some of the women reading this right now are thinking: *This guy is crazy. I can't be seduced!* Unfortunately, women who believe they can't be seduced are the easiest to seduce. They don't guard against it, because they are clueless as to how seduction occurs. Even a woman deeply in love can be seduced. (I will explain this more in a later section.) Other women are probably saying, *Yes, that is exactly what happened to me.*

If you're a man, right now you might be thinking, *No way, not my wife! My wife is a good girl.* Sorry, just because you don't know how does not mean it can't happen. If your wife's love throttle is getting seriously low, it is easy for another man to make regular increases and surpass you. If that happens, she will discover quickly that her sex drive is as high as it ever was, just for a man other than you. This may also cause her to believe the problem is with you. Until she is around someone who triggers it, she may believe that her sex drive is low or gone. Remember: Seventy percent of women and seventy-two percent of men cheat. We're starting to deal with the primary cause of it now.

After conducting her study on married women's sexuality, Michelle Langley wrote a pamphlet on the four stages women go through in marriage. I have some strong issues with Michelle's opinions, and her four stages do not address women who remain faithful in their marriage, but I would still like you to see what she discovered.

Michelle Langley's Women's Infidelity: Stage 1

At this stage, the women I interviewed said that they felt as though something was missing in their lives. They had all the things that they wanted—a home, a family, a great husband— but felt they should be happier. Over time, many of the women noticed a distinct loss of sexual desire; they reported that they were no longer interested in sex. They spent a great deal of energy trying to avoid physical contact with their husbands for fear it might lead to a sexual encounter. They frequently complained of physical ailments to avoid having sex and often tried to avoid going to bed at the same time as their husbands. They viewed sex as a job, not unlike doing the dishes or going to the grocery store. Some of the women claimed that when their husbands touched them, they felt violated; they said their bodies would freeze up and they would feel tightness in their chest and/or a sick feeling in their stomach. The majority of the women in Stage 1 felt there was something wrong with them, that they were in some way defective. They were also fearful that their disinterest in sex would cause their husbands to cheat, or worse yet, leave them.[9]

First, let me state boldly that it is not anyone's fault. There is nothing the husband has done to cause the drop in his wife's sex drive, and there is nothing wrong with the woman either. The good news is, there are things men and women can do to overcome this problem. Langley admits that many women never have an affair. She sees this fidelity as a state of female oppression, because the woman is stuck in what Langley believes is an unnatural monogamous marriage. Since Langley sees monogamy as an oppression of women by men, she does not offer any possible hope for a happy, monogamous marriage. The book is written with a long conversation occurring between herself and a friend named Kevin. In the following excerpt, Kevin begins with a question to her.

Why do you say it can be destructive?

Because, a) women don't know it's coming, and b) women have been taught things about themselves that simply are not true.

Like what?

Namely, that they're naturally monogamous.

---

[9] Michelle Langley (2005) "Why Women Cheat," womensinfidelity.com, accessed March 8, 2016, http://womensinfidelity.com/womens-infidelity-women-why-women-cheat

Are you saying that women aren't naturally monogamous?

Yes, that's exactly what I'm saying. On some level you must realize that we teach girls this myth in order to control their sexual behavior.[10]

Clearly, Michelle believes that monogamy is imposed on women. In fact, she states, "With these things in mind, one could speculate that continuing a sexually exclusive relationship with the same partner for more than four years is unnatural."[11] The question is: What causes this drop in the wife's sex drive?

While engaged, I explained this enigma to my Sweet Paula. She was stunned and replied that she could not imagine that happening in our marriage. I assured her that it would. I wanted her to understand and be prepared to deal with it. I explained my solution and asked if she believed it would work. She agreed. We paid particular attention to her sex drive and our relationship. We were always loving and intimate, yet her drive still declined. She was puzzled and disturbed by this.

Since there is almost nothing written on the subject, few have had the opportunity to study it and see what the underlying causes might be. Perhaps it is a matter of overfamiliarity. One possibility is that she builds a tolerance for her husband's male pheromones, like

---

[10] Michelle Langley (2005), *Women's Infidelity: Living in Limbo*. McCarlan Publishing, p. 18.

[11] Ibid, p. 66.

becoming tolerant to a pain drug when one takes it regularly. Another possibility is it's like getting all the chocolate you can eat; therefore, you don't desire chocolate nearly as much. If you are Christian, I believe you could tie it to original sin. Our inability to find a definitive answer is one reason I call it an enigma.

Tim & Debbie's Downward Spiral

You may recall that after Tim and Debbie got married, they found themselves making love with great intensity almost daily. In fact, there were times when they made love several times a day. Debbie was so happy with Tim that she would brag to her girlfriends about what a wonderful lover Tim was. Tim would get embarrassed whenever Debbie did this, but it also made him feel loved and desired. The two felt like they were so in love they could take on the world and win. Their marriage was off to a wonderful start. Their love throttles were at about ninety percent, and they were deeply in love.

Tim had a high-paying job, and Debbie loved making a beautiful home and taking care of Tim. He had bought her the huge dream home Debbie had always wanted, and she loved it! When Tim came through the door after work, Debbie had a meal on the table, and life was great for both of them. Tim would do his share of chores and help Debbie around the house when needed, and when Debbie was stressed from having too much to do, Tim hired a housekeeper to come in every week to do the deep cleaning.

Tim and Debbie had also found a church they both liked and attended church together twice a week. In time, they became best friends with the pastor and his wife. The two were happy together. Tim would have given Debbie the moon if he could, and Debbie knew it. They both felt as though their lives were exactly the way they should be. They were still making large love throttle increases with each other, and their love throttles were at an all-time high.

Then, as happens in just about every marriage, Debbie's sexual desire for Tim began to wane. The drop was slow and subtle, but Tim noticed it right away. Whenever Tim attempted to make love and Debbie was not in the mood, Tim felt hurt and rejected. Now Debbie was making large and regular decreases from Tim's love throttle.

Tim was puzzled about why he felt so much emotional pain just because Debbie was not in the mood. He thought about it constantly and wondered what to do and why he felt so hurt. *I know she loves me,* Tim reasoned, so *why does this cause me so much emotional pain?*

Without realizing it, Tim started withdrawing emotionally from Debbie. He also talked to Debbie about what was going on and her lack of desire. Tim explained that he knew things would slow down eventually, but Debbie had slowed to such a degree that Tim felt neglected and undesirable. Debbie assured Tim that he was a great guy and that she loved him, but she was at a loss as to why she no longer desired sex. In fact, Debbie said she did not have a sex drive at all like she used to. Despite her reassurances, Tim became depressed.

Tim suggested Debbie make an appointment with her gynecologist to see if there was anything wrong with her, but the gynecologist said Debbie was fine. Although Tim did not want there to be anything seriously wrong with Debbie, he had hoped the doctor would find something that could be corrected easily. When Debbie told Tim there was nothing wrong, Tim's heart sank, because he did not know what to do.

Tim's heart was broken over Debbie's loss of desire for him. Making love with Debbie was some of the best moments of his life. For Tim, nothing compared to having her wrapped lovingly around him. Those moments made Tim feel loved and desired, which made him feel like he could conquer the world for her. Now, without any explanation, the most important part of intimacy in his life had vanished. This caused continued and major love throttle decreases.

As happens when couples enter the downward spiral, issues that they used to deal with easily turned into major disagreements. This problem compounded the tension and heartache. Both of them found they were not as willing to please each other. Tim snapped at Debbie regularly over minor issues, and Debbie fired right back. Debbie was beginning to think that Tim was not the man she thought she had married.

Out of self-preservation, Tim began to withdraw emotionally. He thought that maybe some time apart or perhaps less time together would help, so he started taking the out-of-town work his company offered. As Tim spent two or three weeks away, immersing himself in work, he was able to put his problems with Debbie out of his mind.

When Tim talked to Debbie on the phone, Debbie would tell Tim that she loved and missed him. Everything felt normal, so Tim hoped this time apart was giving Debbie a much-needed break and that she would start to desire him once again. Tim was trying to be logical and find a possible solution to the problem.

In truth, Debbie was unhappy Tim had to do so much work out of town, and she had no idea he had volunteered to take the assignments. Although Debbie missed Tim, she knew he wanted more sex, and she did not know what to do about it. She did not understand that, for Tim, the problem had grown into an explosive and all-consuming issue in their marriage. *After all,* she thought, *it's just sex. Tim just needs to get a grip and settle down. No couple can honeymoon forever.*

Debbie called her trusted friend Mary, who had been married for about six years, to discuss the matter with a woman who had more marriage experience. Mary told Debbie that they only had sex once every week or two. When Debbie heard that, she felt like she was normal and Tim was being unrealistic in his desires for her.

When Tim returned home, he found that nothing had changed. Although Debbie missed Tim, her sexual desire for him had not increased. In fact, Debbie resented Tim's being gone, which made regular love throttle decreases and reduced her sexual desire for him even further. She asked Tim to stay home more, but Tim did not want to stay home, because being around her made him feel frustrated, hurt, and humiliated. He did not express those feelings to Debbie though. He was feeling resentful, and he didn't think she deserved an explanation.

"Would anything be different if I sacrificed at work and stayed home more?" Tim asked.

"I would be happier," Debbie replied.

"Yes," said Tim, "but there wouldn't be any additional sex."

Debbie resented the thought that sex was a strong enough reason to keep Tim home but his love for her and wanting to be with her was not. To Debbie, this made Tim look shallow (more love throttle decreases).

Their marriage had begun a slow and serious downward spiral. Tim was lonely, and so was Debbie. Debbie continued making major decreases to his love throttle, and Tim made major decreases to hers. Finally, Debbie told Tim she did not marry him to live alone most of the time. Tim fired back that he did not get married to live a life of celibacy. Debbie informed Tim that he did not live a life of celibacy, because he did get it sometimes. By that point, they were having sex once every month or two.

"What have I done?" Tim exclaimed. "What great sin have I committed against you that you no longer desire me?" Debbie was stunned as Tim continued. "I work hard. I make an excellent living. I treat you like gold. I don't drink. I don't do drugs, I don't gamble. And I have never cheated on you. So, what exactly have I done to deserve this from you?"

Debbie was crying and furious with Tim for this outburst, but Tim continued, regardless. "What is it about me exactly you find so revolting? Tell me, what I have done to you?"

Debbie was hurt and upset. "Because you are you, and that is more than enough for any woman to ever have to deal with!"

Tim was so shocked by Debbie's response that he walked away wondering if Debbie even loved him anymore. *Why are we married?* Tim wondered. Their marriage was about to go from a downward spiral into a free-fall.

Tim's company had just sold several pieces of large equipment worth over a million dollars, and they asked Tim to head up the installation. The estimated time for the job was three months, and Tim would only be able to return home every second weekend. Tim thought that maybe if Debbie only saw him a couple times a month, she would want him at least that much.

When Tim told Debbie he had been tasked to do the install, Debbie said nothing, but inside, she felt like Tim was deserting her, because she would not give him sex when he wanted it. Debbie began to wonder if that was all Tim had ever wanted. Tim was rarely affectionate, and he did little to make Debbie feel as though he loved her. Debbie felt resentful toward Tim, and there was no way she was going to have sex with him just because he wanted it, especially with his attitude! Now the decreases in both throttles were steady and large.

Once on the job site, Tim was pleased to find he would be working with a capable young woman named Cindy. Not many of Tim's customers had such female talent. On top of that, she was ten years younger than Tim and very attractive.

At first, other than noticing her talent and good looks, Tim had no thoughts of anything else. After all, she was the customer, and he knew others who had got into serious trouble and lost their job for fraternizing with customers.

As time went on, Tim found he was spending a great deal of time with Cindy. In fact, they found working dinners were needed often to discuss and settle problems. Furthermore, Cindy made no secret of the fact she liked Tim (love throttle increases). Conversation turned often to their personal lives, and Tim shared what was happening at home. This just encouraged Cindy to raise the level of flirtation. She seemed shocked that Tim's wife did not want him. She said Tim was quite the catch for any woman, and she could not understand why Debbie was being so foolish. "There's no way my husband would ever have that sort of problem," she said, "not if he was anything like you." (More love throttle increases.)

Cindy began flirting a great deal, trying to raise Tim's spirits and comfort him. Tim did nothing to discourage her, and in time, Tim began to feel close to her. Cindy made Tim feel attractive and desirable (more love throttle increases), things Debbie almost never did anymore.

One evening after dinner, they found themselves looking over blueprints in Tim's hotel room as they tried to solve a problem. Once they had found a solution, Tim realized the position in which he had put himself. It became crystal clear to him that Cindy was ready to make love, so Tim came right out and confronted her.

"You want to make love right now, don't you?"

"Are you that clueless?" Cindy asked.

Tim paused for a moment. He was getting wound up at the thought of being with Cindy. Finally, he shook his head. "I can't. I love Debbie."

Tim knew that spurning Cindy was probably going to have some significant repercussions on customer relations down the road. Sure enough, Cindy left feeling humiliated and embarrassed.

In tears, Tim called Debbie and explained that they had to find a solution to their problem, that he had been tempted and almost slept with Cindy. Tim was reaching out for an emotional life preserver. Instead of helping, Debbie accused him of sleeping with Cindy and told him he was just feeling guilty. Tim denied it, but Debbie didn't believe him and said she would never believe that he had not slept with Cindy.

The relationship went into a tailspin but then leveled out. Tim remained broken, feeling unloved by Debbie and resenting her for withholding sex. Debbie felt bitter towards Tim for his actions as well. However, in time, they both adjusted and became more like friends than lovers. Debbie continued to give Tim sex occasionally, but they never found a way to renew the intimacy they once had.

I Won't Stand for It!

At this point, many men and women feel justified in cheating. If she has been making regular decreases to his love throttle and he has been making decreases to hers, either or both spouses might become so lonely, angry, and bitter that they feel justified in having an affair with someone else. It's not hard for either to rationalize that they are entitled to have their basic needs met. The husband often finds himself struggling emotionally and physically with temptations he would never consider otherwise. If there is a nice looking and interesting man in her life, the wife might as well.

Both might know other people waiting in the wings who are interested in them. Remember, his wife thought he was wonderful, too, when she married him. He thought she was worth making love to for the rest of his life. Yet, even if neither decides to cheat, they are vulnerable and may not realize it. Remember: Statistics show that over seventy-two percent of men cheat on their wives and over seventy percent of women cheat on their husbands. A woman may believe she has the reins well in hand when it comes to her husband getting sex, but she is foolish for believing that! He may believe she would never sleep with anyone but him, but he is also foolish to accept that as a fact! They are even more foolish for not taking care of each other's needs. The unforeseen reactions could be devastating to their marriage.

Now that I have identified this problem, I want to talk about the next enigma so that you can begin to understand the true magnitude of the problem here. If the woman's and the man's enigmas are not dealt with properly, a third enigma can surface that can complicate relations further and destroy the marriage. But first things first.

6

THE SECOND ENIGMA

If there is an area I find women believe they understand their husband, it is his sex drive. Most women find their man wants sex far more than they do, so they believe their husband is oversexed. This is almost a universal belief among women. Of course, they do not think this on their honeymoon. Such thoughts only occur after a woman's drive begins to diminish. Who changed, him or her? Everyone reading this knows the wife changed first, yet she will proclaim boldly that her husband is the one with the problem.

As I noted in the chapter on love actions, sex is different for a man in love than for a woman. This knowledge about the husband and wife is critical to understand. Also, let me remind you again of my 70/30 rule: What is true for one spouse is partially true for the other.

A wife needs to feel loved in order to enjoy sex with her husband. However, the act of sex, although intimate for her, does not necessarily make her feel loved. For the wife, sex is primarily that, sex. Key message: The act of sex is not a primary way to make a woman feel loved!

Now, here's the problem: Because sex is not a primary love action for a woman, most wives believe the same is true of their husband. I have often heard women say their husband treats them like "a piece of meat." When a wife speaks this way about her husband's desire, she reveals almost no understanding of the downward spiral of marriage or her husband's need for sex.

Unfortunately, men also fail to understand their own sex drive and what sex means to them or how it affects them. Since most men do not understand their own sex drive, it makes it almost impossible for them to explain it to their wives. This lack of understanding about the male sex drive is the second enigma that contributes to the downward spiral.

The Secret of the Male Sex Drive

Women have little understanding and respect for how men, particularly their husbands, function in this area. Women have been taught they should never have to have sex if they don't want to or if they are not in the mood. It is all about them and what they want. The woman and the woman alone is the gatekeeper, so if she doesn't want sex, too bad for him. This is a foolish view, and the women who hold it probably have a broken husband vulnerable to cheating or falling in love with another woman. Women who believe this may think it gives them power, but it actually diminishes their power instead!

Women think the male sex drive is primarily physical in nature; therefore, it is not important. A great number of women believe men should just exert some self-control. Many women even resent the male sex drive. In fact, many men wish they had no drive at all because of the way their wife makes them feel. Ladies need to understand something important: Without a burning, loving, and consuming sex drive for you, other than children, your husband may not have any reason to be married to you! Trust me when I tell you that he can hire out the rest. Some women may be shocked that I would make such a statement, so let me explain.

Although there is a physical aspect to the male sex drive, for a man in love, *having sex is the primary way he feels loved by his wife.* I cannot emphasize this enough. The man who does not have his most important need met is lonely and, therefore, vulnerable to other females, whether or not he or his wife believes it.

When speaking to me about the birds and the bees when I was a young lad, my dad explained it to me this way: "When a woman and a man fall in love, they want to be as close as they can be with each other. When you make love with your wife, you are getting as close to her as is physically possible. Nothing in the world can compare with the feeling of love you will receive when you make love with her." Dad had it right. When a man has sex with his wife, he feels loved by her. There is nothing better in the world for a husband in love with his wife than to feel her wrapped lovingly around him.

If you're a woman, ask yourself this: Would you want to be married to a man if you did not feel loved by him? Your husband may know in his head that you love him, but his love throttle is getting seriously low if you withhold yourself regularly.

What about when she says no? Shouldn't he just accept it? After all, it's just sex, right? If the woman is not in the mood, why would her husband want to have sex with her? When his wife says no, he feels unloved, rejected, unwanted, unattractive, humiliated, and emotionally devastated. When she says no, especially repeatedly, he feels so unloved that he begins to feel he is unworthy as a husband and a man. This will cause his self-esteem to plunge dramatically. The wife often sees a reaction from her husband but doesn't grasp the true magnitude of her rejection. She may believe his reaction is unjustified, because she is clueless about what he is experiencing emotionally. The magnitude of this emotional kick in the face is astounding. *Every time she says no, she makes major negative pushes on his love throttle.* That includes little comments she might make when he comes to her for it, like, "Really? Again? Wow, are you kidding me? Seriously?" Even a moan of disbelief or disappointment can have this effect.

To put this in perspective, ladies, suppose there was something bothering you a great deal that you needed to share with your husband. You go to talk to your husband, and he says, "You mind if we talk later? I'm not in the mood to talk right now." Later, you come to talk with him, and you can see he is frustrated with you for wanting to talk.

Perhaps something is bothering him, you think, *he has talked to me a lot. He could be having a bad day or have something else on his mind. This is probably minor. Maybe something from work is bothering him.* But still, how are you starting to feel?

Later, you come just to snuggle on the couch, and he pulls away. "Honey, I'm not feeling much like snuggling right now," he says. "It's been a long day, and I need a break." This is a reasonable request on his part, right? No?

The next morning, you come for a hug, and he pulls away again. "Please," he says, "I'm busy getting ready for work right now."

Although his reasons seem valid on the surface, you realize there must be a problem, so you come to him later with a different plan. "Honey, we need to spend some time together so we can talk."

You can see he is irritated by your request, and it is obvious he doesn't want to spend time talking with you. Then he responds with frustration, "Again? Seriously?"

The next day, and the day after that, you can see he has the same attitude. He is hardly speaking with you, and he doesn't want you touching him. You realize he is spending more time at work and coming in late and tired, just to fall in bed and go to sleep. It's obvious he is avoiding spending quality time with you and that he doesn't even want to hug or kiss you.

"Have I done something wrong?" you ask. "You don't want to talk to me, and you're not affectionate towards me anymore." You can see he's annoyed with you again merely for asking the question.

"Nothing's wrong," he says. "I just don't have the same desire for hugs or talking as you. You need to talk way too much! I talked to Bob, and his wife doesn't talk nearly as much as you. It's not normal for anyone to want to talk as much as you do."

As a wife, how does your husband's behavior and attitude make you feel? Are you hurt? Feeling unloved?

Suppose he keeps this up for a week, two weeks, a month, two months, or more? What if this becomes a regular pattern with him? Maybe he decides to throw you a few crumbs now and then and talk to you, but he decides when and how much time you will get.

How would that make you feel? What would you do? Would you continue to be the same sweet, loving woman to him, or would your bitterness and resentment begin to grow? Would you be thrilled you married this jerk or wondering if maybe you didn't really know him and maybe, just maybe, you made a mistake. How long would you take this before it turned into a major problem in your marriage? This is exactly how your husband feels when you rebuff his sexual needs!

This is how it feels to be the average man in a marriage relationship in today's culture; which helps in understanding the magnitude of his enigma. He feels lonely, hurt, unloved, disrespected, and rejected regularly as his wife shows little or no interest in having sex with him except in the rare times when she's in the mood. The man has no control over how he feels any more than the woman does when he rejects her requests for affection or quality time. How does a woman expect her man to respond to this rejection?

The first thing the average man will do is withdraw emotionally as his wife continues to make hefty decreases to his love throttle. This is an act of self-preservation as he begins to wonder if she still loves him. He may know that she does in his head, but in his heart, he feels as though she does not. He may regret marrying her and wonder if this was all a big mistake, even though he may never utter the words. Resentment will grow, whether he expresses it or not, and it will grow faster if he keeps it bottled up.

Meanwhile, the wife is clueless that this is having such a deep emotional impact on her husband, because he is doing his best to suck it up and be a man. Not to mention, he does not understand it himself. When she says it's just sex, he agrees on a logical level, because he doesn't understand why it is having such a deep emotional impact. Most men do not understand it is the primary way they feel loved from their wife, and that is why it hurts so badly.

The problem grows larger and larger, yet because so few men understand their own emotions, there is little chance they can explain these feelings to their wife. Usually, the husband considers himself pretty good at problem solving; it's what men do. In this case, however, the husband finds himself at a loss. He might think it's wrong to be so hurt over this, but he has no control over the depth of pain he is feeling. Therefore, he lashes out in ways that upset his wife, because she has rejected him in the way he needs to be loved by her the most! She is making regular and substantial decreases to his love throttle. How is he going to treat his wife? Is he going to provide an atmosphere of affection, gentleness, and love? Not likely! Therefore, he begins easing back on her love throttle as well, creating a vicious circle.

Do you remember that sacred trust each placed in the other at the altar? There was a reason for the promises made. For the man, it was to trust in her and to let her alone satisfy his most intimate and personal needs. If she says no to lovemaking, he feels she is violating that sacred trust. His lifelong dreams of marriage are blowing up in his face, and he has no idea what to do about it.

We all need to feel loved by our spouse. For a man, sex is a need in the same way affection or quality time or talking and sharing emotions is for his wife. It impacts the man so deeply that he may even resent her petting the family dog or cat when she is so unwilling to take care of him. She wants to talk, but he is hurting. She wants quality time, and so does he, but he needs it from her in a different way than she needs it from him. She wants affection, but he is craving sex with her so he can feel loved by her. She may find that if she lets him near her, he may come across as only interested in sex when she needs affection. The truth is, he is hurting and starving for her! Each man handles this differently, but none of their reactions are good for the marriage. A serious downward spiral has begun as the couple loses altitude.

Here's something to think about: If you are a Christian woman and withholding yourself from your husband, you are disobeying a direct command from Scripture.

> A wife belongs to her husband instead of to herself, and a husband belongs to his wife instead of to himself. *So don't refuse sex to each other,* unless you agree not to have sex for a little while, in order to spend time in prayer. Then Satan won't be able to tempt

you because of your lack of self-control. (1 Corinthians 7:4–6 CEV)

God tells us that when we do not give ourselves freely to our spouse, our spouse can be tempted. Some Christian women are much more concerned with what they are taught in modern liberal culture or how they feel rather than Scripture. Many will make excuses for why they should not have to fulfill their marital duty.

In response, some men spend more time away from their wife to avoid the hurt and the pain. They hang out with friends, work overtime, or find something to do away from their wife. Other men withdraw into their own little shell. Now the wife might even feel like her husband is being a jerk without just cause, because she has no clue he has become bitter over her rejection of him. He makes substantial decreases from her love throttle as well, but he probably does not know why and may not even care, because he is hurting so badly. The downward spiral continues to worsen.

This is the time when men are prone to do dumb things that are destructive to their marriage. Trust me, been there, done that several times! The truth is, when men do the stupid things, they are usually so bitter they suppress the fact that the bitterness is because they love and need their wife so much. He may find himself tempted and doing things he never would have considered otherwise. At this point, a man's actions can be self-defeating and destructive for the marriage if he doesn't pull himself together.

Eventually, something happens that leads to a serious argument, maybe over an unrelated subject. Things blow up to the point that the relationship itself is threatened, and then the couple makes up and makes passionate love, "makeup sex," But they still have not addressed the enigmas in their marriage, so they go right back to where they were before they started arguing. The downward spiral resumes, this time from a lower altitude. If this condition continues, eventually, both spouses will be ripe for an affair. It would not require much effort for someone to start making large increases to either spouse's love throttle. The marriage, now spiraling out of control, may go into a free fall.

At this point, a large number of marriages level off, but often at a dangerously low altitude. This can last from a few weeks to several years. The couple becomes more like friends than lovers. He does not approach her for sex nearly as often, if at all, because his spirit has been broken. His wife may even come to believe sex is not that important to him. He buries his pain and goes on. He "man's up," so to speak. Perhaps there are children to consider. If they are Christians, church responsibilities or what friends or family will think might also cause them to accept their situation. The couple might start believing their marriage is healthy and normal. Since the husband has no control over his wife, he feels he has no good options. He may start lying to himself and deny that being with his wife is important to him. Although he may suck it up and move on, the problem continues to grow.

Once a couple settles into this pattern, they might begin to believe they have gotten over the worst part or that they have a good marriage. I have seen this countless times. This happens a great deal in Christian marriages. Yet he is open to foolish temptations now and could behave in ways contrary to the well-being of the marriage. Both are vulnerable to an affair and don't realize it. Why do you suppose so many Christian ministers end up falling? Everyone, including the minister, thought he and his spouse had a good marriage. These couples are vulnerable though, because their needs are being neglected. Pastors also have it harder, because women often target them.

I have known several ministers and some ministers' wives who ended up in an affair even though they believed their marriage was healthy. Yet, inquiries about the level of intimacy in their marriage revealed it was sadly lacking. Their marriage had gone through the downward spiral several times until it leveled off, but neither spouse knew how to improve their situation. Many had no idea marriage could be better. The wife was in complete control of the couple's sex life, and she alone determined how much he needed.

Sometimes a husband will keep his mouth shut and take what she is willing to give, fearing he might lose that as well. Yet, he will still feel resentful. If the husband stays faithful, he might find himself questioning whether to get out of the marriage when he hits midlife. This is why men have midlife crises. They falsely believe a younger woman will have a higher sex drive. Do they want what they have now (no sex or almost no sex) for the rest of their life, or should they bail out while there's still a chance for real happiness (making love) with someone else?

When a woman finds her husband is having midlife crisis, she will usually do what is needed for a while to get him through it. This is a deception though. The sex she gives him will not last, because it does not come from the heart, but from a fear of losing him.

7

THE THIRD ENIGMA

When a couple goes on without solving the downward spiral of marriage, both are ripe for an affair, whether they believe it or not. Earlier, I stated that Willard F. Harley, Jr. reports that religious beliefs matter little when it comes to affairs. The only ingredient needed for an affair to begin is for a person of worth to come into a spouse's life and begin making regular love throttle increases.

Although the wife may not realize it, she is just as vulnerable as her husband to an affair. An affair requires just one simple equation: a downward spiral until a spouse's love throttle is low or almost in neutral + an attractive person who makes enough regular increases in the spouse's love throttle + opportunity = affair every time!

The relationship with the affair partner usually begins with friendship. Things start out innocently, but over time, love throttle increases are made. Soon, a spouse begins to feel a strong attraction to someone other than his or her partner.

Some couples have good ground rules in place that make an affair much harder to start. But even the best rules will not inoculate a person who is lonely and longing for intimacy. And remember: affairs are the leading cause of divorce.

A partner begins feeling good when the other person is around, because that person makes regular love throttle increases. Over time, they share more of their lives and find they feel close to each other emotionally. They look forward to seeing each other and talking together. Then, maybe without even realizing how vulnerable they are, the friends begin to hug occasionally for support. Then comes the right opportunity and a hug that leads magically to passionate lovemaking, and the affair has begun.

Amy & Frank

When I met Amy and Frank, they seemed like a happy couple. One day, Amy came to me for some marital advice. When I inquired about how much sex she was having with Frank, she confessed she gave him little. Frank was a good looking man, and I warned Amy she could be in for some rough times ahead if she did not take care of Frank's needs. I also explained how important it is for a man to have sex with his wife to feel loved by her. Any man whose wife does not meet his needs regularly feels rejected and unloved by her. He could become bitter as well and may feel justified in having sex with another woman. Amy assured me they were happy and that she had the situation well in hand. She told me Frank loved her so much he would never fool around on her.

A short while later, I received a phone call from Amy. She was in tears. She had discovered Frank was having an affair. There was no point in saying, "I told you so," because she knew.

She tried to get Frank to break things off. She realized her mistake and gave him a lot of sex. Unfortunately, Frank's new lover had been making increases to Franks love throttle for some time, and he had fallen in love with her. Although Frank tried, he found he could not stay away from her. She was in the field working with him three or four times a week. When Amy realized Frank was not going to stop his affair, she filed for divorce.

Was there anything Amy could have done differently to get Frank to end his affair? The answer is *yes*. Even after a man has become bitter towards his wife, he still loves her and wants to make things work. He only needs her to love him in the way every man needs to be loved.

I hope you never find yourself in this situation, but if this describes your circumstances, you will need to take drastic measures. I will discuss this in detail later.

It could just as easily have been Amy in the affair. She also found herself tempted by a man she knew, but there was never the right opportunity for her to cheat. A woman's affair can be much more serious, because she will usually fall in love with the affair partner and decide to leave the marriage relationship believing she has finally met the right guy. Generally, the man does not feel this way about his affair partner. I will reveal why shortly.

Sometimes when a woman is involved in an affair, she will want space. If she feels as though she could be falling in love with her affair partner, she might ask her husband for a separation, but she will not tell him about the affair. She finds herself confused and unable to make a decision about what to do. She loves her husband and believes he does not deserve this, but why should she stay and not have such a wonderful man in her life? This is part of what Michelle Langley calls "limbo." Here is how she describes it.

Women's Infidelity: Stage 2

Women at Stage 2 experienced reawakened desire stimulated by encounters outside the marital relationship. Whether the new relationships involved sex or remained platonic, they were emotionally significant to these women. Many of the women had felt no sexual desire for a long time. Many experienced tremendous guilt and regret, regardless of whether their new relationships were sexual, merely emotional, or both. Most experienced what could be termed an identity crisis—even those who tried to put the experience behind them. Constant reminders were everywhere. They felt guilt when the topic of infidelity arose, whether in the media, in conversations with family and friends, or at home with their husbands. They could no longer express their prior disdain for infidelity without feeling like hypocrites. They felt as though they had lost a part of themselves. Reflecting society's belief that women are either "good" or "bad," these women questioned their "good girl" status and felt that they might not be deserving of their husbands. Many tried to overcome feelings of guilt by becoming more attentive toward and appreciative of their husbands. However, over time the predominant reaction of a number of the women moved from appreciation to justification. In order to justify their continued desire for other men, they began to attribute those desires to needs that were not being met in the marriage, or to their husband's past behavior. Many became negative and sarcastic when speaking of their husbands and their marriages. In many cases, an extramarital affair soon followed.[12]

Affair Sex

Once a wife becomes engaged in an affair, she makes an amazing discovery: affair sex is mind-blowing—for a while. I refer to this as "the third enigma." Almost no one knows about it, or at least no one talks about it. If her new lover is skilled in lovemaking, she may find sex with him is immensely better than any sex

---

[12] Michelle Langley (2005) "Why Women Cheat," womensinfidelity.com, accessed March 8, 2016, http://womensinfidelity.com/womens-infidelity-women-why-women-cheat

she ever had with her husband. It doesn't matter if her husband is drop-dead gorgeous and a spectacular lover. She finds herself reaching sexual peaks with the new lover that she did not even know were possible.

Harley writes that wives in affairs report "a degree of ecstasy, otherwise unknown to her in marriage that lacks affection."[13] He believes this is because of the extra affection she receives from the affair partner. I disagree strongly and will explain why shortly. The important point is the wife reporting sex with someone other than her husband is the best sex she has ever had.

Michelle Langley compares affair sex to a type of drug because of its intensity. I believe once a woman experiences it, she is hooked, because she falsely believes the ecstasy she is feeling is due to something particular about the affair partner. This is how a woman ends up in "limbo," unable to decide between her lover and her husband. Langley, although identifying affair sex as addictive, dismisses (Tracey) her example woman, as not really understanding what she is experiencing: "Things are causing changes in her brain chemistry. With these wide ranging feelings of fear and excitement Tracey could be stoned out of her mind. Though she may believe that she is experiencing something entirely new." [14]

When Langley refers to being stoned out of her mind, she is referring to the level of ecstasy women experience in affair sex.

---

[13] Ibid

[14] Ibid

"Falling in love may not be the high of all highs, but falling in love when you are already married may very well be. Affairs may be the 'crack high' of natural acts."[15]

Affair sex can be so spectacular the woman thinks she has finally met Mr. Right because of the way it makes her feel. She may even think he is her soul mate, because he can drive her to such high levels of ecstasy. She is certain the sex is so good because he is so wonderful. This self-deception is common, because women aren't educated on what is happening to them and fail to understand their own sex drive. But how could she be educated about it when no one knows or wants to talk about it?

The truth is the great and wonderful intensity of the sex she is experiencing has little to do with any particular man. It is due to the incredibly erotic stimulation she has when she has sex with a man other than her husband. It's the situation that arouses her, not any particular individual.

For most women, sex is just that, sex, but the third enigma is that sex with a man other than her husband is simply the most erotic sex possible for a woman. Some women experience such spectacular eroticism it can be almost impossible to break things off, especially if there is an emotional connection. Many women believe they are in love, because the sex is so amazing, and they have no frame of reference to help them understand that great sex without love is possible.

---

[15] Ibid

To give you some idea of the truth concerning sex and women, think about some of the movies that are rated by women as romantic or erotic. Many women love the movie *Unfaithful* starring Richard Gere. It is the story of a happily married woman being seduced by a guy who is good looking and somewhat of a player. In the movie, he sweeps her off her feet and carries her to bed. She tries to resist him, but she can't and surrenders to the lure of his seduction. Even though she feels horrible in the beginning for cheating, the sex is so good she finds herself returning to him over and over again. The sex is great for her, and many women can relate instinctively to what that might be like, which is a major reason why women like the movie.

Another movie, termed by women as a "beautiful love story," is *The Bridges of Madison County* with Clint Eastwood as the male lover. In this film, a woman in an average marriage falls in love with a visiting photographer while her husband and children are away at the state fair. It doesn't start out as an affair, but as the two spend time together, they become more and more attracted to each other until they are making passionate love. She does not leave her husband, but the film portrays the affair partner as the one true love of her life. Staying with her husband, although the right thing to do, is portrayed as a major sacrifice.

Why do so many women find these movies alluring? In *Unfaithful,* there is the irresistible seduction. Women can relate to the eroticism the woman experiences during the seduction. Most women understand that with the right man, such a seduction is like a fantasy come true. The lovemaking with the affair partner was incredible. The way the woman in the movie reacted to the seduction was extremely realistic, and every woman who watches it knows it. In *The Bridges of Madison County,* the wife was in a mediocre marriage, which helped women relate to her and empathize with her. This also helped the movie come across as a beautiful love story, a realistic portrayal of how affairs like this could occur. Both movies portrayed wives having great sex with a man other than their husband. My point is, there is often no requirement of love for a woman to have spectacular sex. Many women may disagree with me here, but the evidence proves them wrong.

Case in point: An entire publishing industry is based around erotic stories for women. In 2014, erotica was reported to be a $1.4 billion industry.[16] We used to call them romance novels, but they are really the equivalent of female porn. If women didn't find these books sexually stimulating, why would they read them? Also, if the women who disagree with me are correct, there would never be a female seduction and no players.

Another proof of this is women who practice the "hot wife" lifestyle. They report having the best sex ever with their affair partners without feeling any love towards them. Another common example of sex just being sex for women is the one-night stand. Many women go out to clubs in search of a man. Although it

---

[16] Claire Siemaszkiewicz (January 7, 2014) "Yes, Yes, Yesssss…! Erotic Romance Sales Still Sizzle." Publishingperspectives.com, accessed March 9, 2016, http://publishingperspectives.com/2014/01/yes-yes-yesssss-erotic-romance-sales-still-sizzle/#.VtNQEI-cFev

may not be her plan to have sex that evening, it happens often, and no one can honestly say they fell in love dancing together that night. Then we have friends with benefits. No love or commitment needed; just good sex. As I said, the evidence proving that women do not require love to have good sex is overwhelming.

By saying all of this, I don't mean to criticize women or to glorify affair sex. After all, as time passes, any woman who leaves her husband for the new lover will discover she is in the same spot once again. If she marries her new lover, the same loss of desire for him will occur, just as it did for her first husband. However, this time the fall from her peak will be much greater, because she falsely believed it would be different this time. Rather than criticize or point fingers, my intention is to help both men and women understand the truth about the male and the female sex drive and how failure to understand these enigmas can lead people to misunderstand the third enigma, affair sex. Once you understand these enigmas and why they happen, you will be in a position to take the actions needed to create a healthy and happy marriage.

But before we move on to that, I have a bit more to say about another difficult topic: seduction.

8

FEMALE SEDUCTION REVEALED

When asked, almost all women claim they could never be seduced. Women feel they have control and that they could never be compelled to do anything they did not want to do. Then there are men who see female seduction as an art form. So, the question arises, who is right? How can a man get a woman to behave in a manner she denies is possible, especially when she's married? The following story will illustrate how this can occur. But first, a quick word about players.

Players

In my teens and twenties, I had a friend who was an unbelievable player. Not only was he a drop-dead gorgeous hunk, he knew how to seduce women. It was stunning to watch him land woman after woman. Occasionally, we would make bets on whether he could seduce a particular woman. Generally, she was a stranger to both of us, or at least to him, because I only bet when I believed it was almost impossible for him to win. But he collected just about every time. I watched him get a severe beating twice by husbands whose wives he had seduced. It didn't matter if she was a Christian woman either. If he wanted her, he got her. Married or single made no difference to him. As a result, I didn't allow any of the girls I dated to be alone with him or I would break up with them on the spot. He moved out of state when I was about twenty-five, and I haven't seen or heard from him since, but I know someone else who also had a friend who was a successful player. There are far more of these guys around now due to all the information available about seduction. If you don't believe me, just do a search online. Now, let's look at a player in action.

Debbie's Seduction

Three years into Tim and Debbie's marriage, they had gone through several downward spirals, but things had leveled off, and they believed their marriage was pretty good. They had developed a solid friendship, even though there was not much sex.

Debbie had never been with anyone other than her husband. When Debbie met Tim's friend Mike though, she thought, *that is one good looking man.* Mike was cheerful, and Debbie laughed at his jokes. He had a great smile, and it felt good to be around someone like him who was so happy (love throttle increases). Mike would comment on how lucky Tim was to have such a beautiful wife (more love throttle increases). Debbie would get a little embarrassed, but it felt good to hear it. Sometimes when Mike called for Tim, Debbie answered the phone, and Mike would say something like, "Hello, beautiful" or "How's the gorgeous woman of the house?" These compliments made Debbie feel good (love throttle increases), but it seemed like harmless flirting.

Soon, Mike began to feel like a friend to Debbie. Mike and Debbie hugged when Mike came over and again when he left (more love throttle increases). Debbie enjoyed Mike's hugs, and she wished Tim would hug her more (decreases for Tim).

Mike always listened attentively to Debbie, and Debbie could tell Mike cared about her feelings. She was glad to have a friend like Mike with whom she could talk (love throttle increases). Why couldn't Tim be more attentive to her?

The truth is, Mike knew something that Tim did not: When a woman is allowed to share her feelings and problems with a man, it makes her feel like the man cares about her.

Soon, Mike and Debbie were feeling comfortable around each other, and it was nothing for Mike to hug her or give her a pat on the back (love throttle increases). One time he came over when Debbie was sad, and he spent a little extra time empathizing with her and hugging her (love throttle increases). Debbie loved how Mike's hugs made her feel, even though she found they were starting to arouse her, but she knew no one else knew she was aroused, so she figured it was harmless. After all, she would never let anything like *that* happen.

Tim didn't mind Mike and Debbie's friendship at all. He knew he had married a faithful woman who would never cheat, so he had no need to worry about her. Not only that, Tim knew her sex drive was down so much she barely wanted sex anymore. Tim reasoned that since he would never consider cheating on Debbie, why would Debbie, who had little or no sex drive, consider cheating on him? Tim was confident there was no reason to worry.

Michelle Langley's research shows this complete trust from husbands is common and gives women unbelievable freedom to carry on an affair right under their husband's nose. She reports that some of the women referred to their husbands as stupid for being so naïve: "What's interesting is that although females never give males any indication that they are anything less than 100 percent faithful, females seem to think males are stupid for believing them."[17] Isn't it a sad state of affairs when a woman thinks her husband is stupid for trusting her and believing in her?

After several downward spirals, women often feel bitter toward their husbands. They justify these feelings because of how they have been treated. The wife has no clue about the real reason for his bitterness and simply returns his resentment. She becomes convinced it's his fault and that he's a jerk and then uses this logic to justify her behavior. She is able to rationalize that it's her husband's fault, because he has neglected her. Hence, he is stupid to believe she won't get her needs met elsewhere.

In truth, Mike had an unscrupulous and sordid history. He was an experienced player and loved the challenge of seducing married women. He seemed to have a natural ability to read a woman. He knew their

---

[17] Michelle Langley (2005) "Why Women Cheat," womensinfidelity.com, accessed March 8, 2016, http://womensinfidelity.com/womens-infidelity-women-why-women-cheat

smiles when he gave them certain looks and watched them react to his compliments. He knew female body language and gauged his possibilities by how a woman responded to particular comments. Mike had read a great deal on seduction and female body language. For example, he knew that when he complimented a woman and she stroked her face or brushed back her hair, subconsciously, she was sending the message that she found him attractive. He did not even need the woman to flirt back to seduce her, although he had a higher success rate when they did. And Mike reveled in the fact that Debbie did flirt with him. As soon as there was an opportunity, Mike planned to make love to her. He would do his best to wow Debbie in bed so she would want to be with him again.

Mike had done a good deal of research and had discovered an abundance of information about seducing married women. Now he was having great success applying these principles. For Mike, it was a thrill to get a committed woman to take him. He had read about how married women could go crazy with another guy. Then he experienced firsthand how a married woman reacted to having a man other than her husband, and he loved it! He found they became much more aroused than any of the single women he had been with.

Mike had also spent a great deal of time learning how to please a woman in bed. In fact, almost every woman he slept with told him he was the best lover they had ever had. Mike was proud to hear those words and even prouder to be a successful player. He had great confidence in his ability to seduce and please women.

While he was seducing Debbie, he was sleeping with two other married women and was looking forward to adding Debbie to his list. She was especially beautiful, and she would be the first married woman he had had who had never been with anyone other than her husband. Mike saw her as the crown jewel, a true accomplishment, and he wanted her badly.

Finally, his big chance came. Due to an ice buildup, Debbie could not get the back patio door to close properly. She called Tim, and Tim, who was on the road, called Mike. Would he mind taking a look at it?

Mike was thrilled! He went into the bathroom to shave and put on some cologne. He laughed to himself as he thought about how easy this would be. Tim was handing Debbie to him on a silver platter. Mike knew Tim had left Sunday, so Debbie had not any sex in at least three days. The truth was, it had been six weeks since Tim and Debbie had made love.

Debbie had no idea what Mike was thinking, but she was a little scared, because she knew she would be alone with him, and that made her feel a bit vulnerable. She was glad he would be fixing her problem and happy to have his company, but she knew they would hug, and that stirred her even more since they would be alone together. Debbie took comfort in the fact there was no way Mike could know this. She thought about how she knew she could trust Mike, and that eased her mind.

An Important Note!

I told you in the beginning that this book was going to have frank, adult conversation about the male and female sex drive and why things happen. As an author though, I face a dilemma here. The next part was written to help women understand how seduction occurs so they can protect themselves from unscrupulous men. There are websites, books, articles, and classes on how to seduce married women. Women who understand how it occurs can protect themselves. I understand some in the Christian community may feel this type of writing crosses the line. However, going deeper and revealing this truth is the only way to help women understand and prevent seduction. If my writing is not bold, women will not understand the magnitude of the problem and may not take the required steps to protect themselves. The truth is, a woman who is not having regular sex with her husband is extremely vulnerable to a player's seduction! If you are offended reading about a seduction and learning how it occurs, please skip the rest of this section and go to "Continue Reading Here." Also, if you are reading this book in a group, I recommend letting each woman read the following section in private. Groups should also skip forward to "Continue Reading Here."

> When Mike got to Debbie's house, he gave Debbie an especially strong hug. He moved his hands affectionately around her back as they hugged. He had never done that before, and he knew this would get her mind wandering. While taking his sweet time looking at

the door, he also entered Debbie's personal space regularly, pausing and giving her that contagious smile of his. Each time he did, Debbie felt close to him and smiled back. This stirred her, which made her a bit nervous, but she liked it, too. Plus, she knew he couldn't possibly know what she was feeling. The truth is, Mike knew exactly what he was doing and how it was making her feel.

At one point, he asked for a hair dryer and used it to melt the ice blocking the jam. He had solved her problem. Then Mike gave Debbie another strong hug, moving his hands up and down her back. But this time he pulled away abruptly. He turned his back to Debbie, took a couple of steps, and straightened himself up. Mike knew that Debbie would know exactly what he was doing, and he wanted her to think about what was happening to him and the fact he needed to make "an adjustment."

Debbie began to laugh.

Mike turned and grinned at her. "So, you think this is funny?"

Still laughing, she nodded. Mike began to chuckle a little, too.

"Well," he said, "that's the effect you have on me. You're so beautiful I can't stop thinking about what it would be like to be with you."

Mike had read several romance novels and knew that, for a woman, it's a matter of her mind. He knew that by making the statement he did, he had taken control of Debbie's thoughts, causing her to think about what it would be like and how it would feel to have him. He knew that when she imagined his words, she would have a reflexive reaction, causing her to feel stimulated and wound up inside.

Still grinning, Debbie shook her head in disbelief that Mike was revealing his personal thoughts to her, but Mike understood women. Debbie had been touching herself regularly since he got there, which told Mike she desired him.

As Debbie laughed, Mike walked over and stood beside her. Then he turned toward her, put his arm around her as if he was going to hug her from the side, but then pulled her tightly against him. He pushed against her hip firmly.

"You think what you do to me is funny?"

As Mike pressed against her, Debbie felt her body's uncontrollable and overwhelming response. She was already breathing harder when he finished the sentence.

"Do you know how good it would feel?"

Once again, he caused Debbie to imagine his words, and the thought stimulated her even stronger inside. She seemed like she was almost in a trance, and Mike knew this was his moment. He reached for the button on her pants. From that point on, it was game over for Debbie. She was his now. Mission accomplished.

For Debbie, this was passionate lovemaking. Mike was at least five times the lover Tim ever hoped to be.

"That was amazing," she gasped afterwards, "absolutely amazing! What did you do to me?"

"I lost control," he said. "You're so beautiful; you make me crazy for you."

Afterwards, Mike stood at the door, holding Debbie and loving on her. He rubbed her back gently as he kissed her cheeks, her chin, her forehead, and her nose. He wanted Debbie to feel like she was special to him.

When Mike left, Debbie was amazed at what she had just experienced. How come making love with Mike was so great? When Debbie asked Mike again what he had done to her, he told her it's just the way we are together. Mike didn't want her to know there were specific things he did that her husband could learn to do as well, if he only knew about them.

Debbie felt horrible that she had cheated on Tim, but this new experience was so incredible it consumed her thoughts. It wasn't long before she found herself in Mike's arms again and again.

Continue Reading Here

The scenario I just gave you depicted a player in action. Most women, however, begin an affair gradually by spending a great deal of time talking to the other man. He begins making numerous increases to her love throttle, perhaps without even realizing it. In time, she feels close to him. Hugs as greetings and departures become normal. Then one day they hug, and it just happens. They are not sure how they ended up in bed together; it just seemed so natural.

In regular affair sex, the level of eroticism or sexual high is almost as strong as the player's seduction. If the man has good lovemaking skills, the husband can be at an insurmountable disadvantage.

This is important to know, because women usually initiate the divorce, and this helps explain why! If she isn't cheating, when she catches her husband cheating repeatedly, which happens sometimes, she loses confidence he will ever be faithful to her. She begins to believe she can never be happy with him. The boredom with her husband, combined with his cheating, can be enough for her to want a divorce. In the majority of cases, however, it is the sexual high she experiences with the new man that clinches it. This makes her feel like she is deeply in love with the affair partner. The majority of women who are in an affair falsely believe their new relationship will lead to a great marriage. As I said, the fall with the new man will be greater, because she is starting out from a higher place, and the expectations will be higher. Boredom with the second man is just as bad as the first. So in the end, the heartache and destruction of destroying a lifetime relationship didn't help. All of this happened because of the enigmas of marriage that no one understood.

Up to this point, we have dealt with the unseen forces that destroy intimacy in marriage. I know that for many men and women, the realization of the enigmas has been extremely painful. Now this book will turn toward describing how to overcome these enigmas and achieve or restore lasting love, intimacy, and joy in your marriage.

9

A Solid Foundation

A great marriage must begin with a common understanding and agreement about what marriage is. This chapter will help you understand how to create such a solid foundation. Then we will go on to look at how to build on this foundation to overcome the enigmas and construct a solid marriage.

Covenant Marriage

To have a successful marriage today, I believe you must have a covenant-style marriage. As designed by God, marriage was always intended to be a blood covenant. What does that mean? What exactly is a covenant agreement? Historically, a covenant agreement was the most solemn and binding agreement possible between two people, tribes, or nations.

I took a course at Vision International Bible College on blood covenants. The textbook was *The Blood Covenant of God* by Pastor Dennis Plant. Although his book was not written specifically about marriage, many of the principles, traditions, and ceremonies it mentions apply.

In ancient times, blood covenants were used to seal peace agreements between peoples and nations. Blood covenants involved a ceremony that announced what vows would be taken and which curses would happen to the partner who broke the covenant. Such covenants involved a solemn pledge of total commitment and loyalty. Both parties pledged to defend the other in every way, never speaking badly of the covenant partner. Each covenant partner would heap praise on the other and announce a willingness to die for the partner if the need arose.

During the ceremony, the covenant partners would walk in a figure-eight pattern around the halves of a slain animal. As they walked, they pronounced curses that described what would happen to them if they broke the covenant agreement. Each partner tried to surpass the other in curses that would happen to them should they break the agreement. Part of the curse always included death to the person who broke the agreement and curses on him in the afterlife. Blessings were also granted for keeping the covenant. Each person also took turns pronouncing his commitment and devotion to the covenant partner. They would shout out compliments and praises. The property owned by each person would also belong to his covenant partner. The covenant lasted until death.

Without a doubt, the blood covenant was the most binding agreement ever between two people. In a covenant agreement, all other people were placed in a subservient role to the covenant partner, who reigned supreme as the highest priority in the life of each party to the agreement.

In the same way, marriage, as intended by God, is a blood covenant between two people. This can become quite literal. Providing the woman is a virgin, there is a literal shedding of blood in the wedding bed. Regardless of whether or not the wife is a virgin, marriage is a sacred covenant between two people, the most solemn agreement two people can make. Think about these words for a moment: "Therefore a man shall leave his father and his mother and shall become united and cleave to his wife, and they shall become one flesh." (Genesis 2:24, AMP). We do not fully understand the way we become one flesh with our marriage partner. However, thinking of your partner as part of yourself helps to bring a fresh perspective on the depth of love, commitment, and devotion needed for a deeply intimate marriage. Each spouse depends on and relies on the devotion of his or her partner. Your partner is entitled to your complete and unfettered devotion, loyalty, support, and tender, never-ending love. If you are not willing to make this commitment to your spouse, you will end up divorced or miserable and maybe both.

My own marriage vows contained the following line from the Bible: "May the Lord deal with me, be it ever so severely, if anything but death separates you and me" (Ruth 1:17b, NIV). Notice the call to "deal ever so severely with me." This vow asks God to curse the one who leaves the marriage for anything short of death. Paula insisted on this vow. I gave some serious thought to those words before agreeing. She wanted serious covenant vows to show the depth of our commitment to each other. It reminded me of covenant agreements throughout history and how seriously those making the vows took them. In the end, I was overjoyed that she wanted such a strong covenant agreement with me.

A covenant agreement is a covenant until death. It doesn't last merely until you're tired of the other person, no longer in love, or you feel the other person has let you down or broken a vow. You cannot break the covenant because you want another "honey" either. If you are married to a person who is not abusive, a sociopath, or a psychopath, the commitment is for life! Does this mean you are committed to be miserable for the rest of your life? No. It means you need to change relations with your partner to build the loving, gentle, and kind marriage God wants you to have.

I know many reading this will think, "But he has no idea how bad this is!" I pastored a church for over ten years. Trust me when I say there is nothing you can tell me about your marriage that I have not heard already. As long as you have a willing partner, your marriage can be restored to happiness and joy. Have patience. The solutions are coming!

Marriage is a Sacred Trust

Your Partner's Needs

When we commit to marry someone, we agree to let that person and that person alone be the sole provider of our most personal needs, wants, and desires. Often, until we are married, we have no idea what that will involve or the depth of commitment and work it will require from us. Yet, without this commitment, we cannot have a happy marriage. *This commitment is absolute and without question.* If we cannot make this commitment and keep it, we have no business getting married. Did I mention "work"? The commitment is not just to let your marriage partner fulfill your needs and desires but also for you to meet your partner's needs and desires. This is not to be taken lightly. Each partner has genuine needs. As I said before, if you do not take this commitment seriously and respect the sacred trust by fulfilling your responsibilities, you will either be miserable, divorced, or both. No one is a rock that can withstand his or her most personal needs not being met. Even if you believe you can, or your partner tells you he or she is that rock, it simply isn't true.

For now, it's important to understand that only your partner can determine his or her needs. It's not your decision. Nothing is as humiliating as one spouse deciding what the other partner needs.

Secrets and Personal Things

Part of the sacred trust of marriage is to be your partner's place to share his or her most personal information, thoughts, feelings, fantasies, and secrets. Your partner needs to know absolutely and without fear that you will never tell anyone or use any information shared in secret against him or her. If you want to destroy any intimacy you have with your partner, just start revealing your partner's deepest secrets, thoughts, and desires to others. This is a betrayal of their sacred trust on a high level and should never happen. Marriages need this deep level of trust so true intimacy can flourish.

People often remark at the stark truth they hear children speak. Art Linkletter had a television show for eighteen years based on this reality called *Kids Say The Darndest Things*. Children often feel free to speak without a filter; it's who they are. In the same way, every marriage partner needs to be able to let his or her "inner child" spring forth in the marriage relationship. When I see the little girl showing herself plainly in my wife, I am moved to tears sometimes, because it brings such joy to my heart. Usually, she is not even aware she's doing something that is touching me so deeply. Without our deep level of intimacy, I would never see that. Intimacy is a true joy when two people share it together without fear.

This is an area of your marriage that you need to nourish and protect. If you are questioning how to be that partner, start by thinking about the priest and the confessional. When someone goes into the confessional and confesses his or her sins, the priest has a sacred trust with the confessor. The priest has made a solemn vow to the Church and to God to never reveal what is shared. It is held to the highest standard of secrecy. If you need or want to share something with someone else, get your partner's permission first. After all, it's your partner's secret, not yours.

Honesty

Honesty is the cornerstone of the marriage relationship. It is just about impossible to build and maintain intimacy in your marriage without honesty. Some people have turned lying into an art form, and they revel in their ability to deceive others. This is a recipe for the destruction of intimacy. Lying is difficult to recover from. If lying becomes a pattern, intimacy will be destroyed. Understanding this is paramount.

Occasionally, everyone fudges the truth a little. Unfortunately, it is part of being human. Sometimes we just let it slip by us, and then there are times when we plan to do it. However, once we discover our partner has lied to us, we feel a breach of the sacred trust. It is one thing to conceal a surprise birthday party or some other surprise event. It is another to deceive your partner because you are keeping a secret you should not be keeping. Even a special surprise can backfire. You should discuss this with your partner. Let me share one of my own mistakes by way of example.

The week I asked Paula to marry me, I carried out an elaborate deception to surprise her. We had talked about getting married, but I had not proposed officially. The ring she loved was more money than I had at the time. She knew that, which helped the deception. Yet, the truth was, I had received a major influx of cash that I did not tell her about.

The deception began the week of Valentine's Day. We were scheduled to go out for dinner on Valentine's Day, and I didn't want her to know I had big plans, so each day in the week leading up to it, I gave her a ring. The first day I gave her a ruby ring. The next day, I gave her a sapphire ring and so on. We refer to it now as "ring week," as she received a new ring every day for a week. They were not expensive rings, but they were nice. On Valentine's Day, I hired a musician to come in at just the right moment after dinner and sing her a love song before I proposed.

One of the ways I deceived her was to give her a final ring at dinner as well as matching earrings and a necklace. All contained her favorite stone. That way she would think they were the big gift of the day. I had also hired a photographer/videographer to record the moment. The whole scenario was difficult to pull off, because the photographer needed to slip me a device to record the musician and our conversation.

On cue, the singer came over and started singing the love song. Paula had no idea what was about to happen, but the song moved her to tears. Immediately afterwards, I fell on one knee and recited a poem that had a proposal at the end. She said yes, but after recovering her faculties the first words out of her mouth were, "You lied to me! You lied to me!"

She was right. I had kept information from her about the money that had come in for the ring. A lie of omission is still a lie.

Even though I had done it to surprise her with a proposal of marriage, she felt deceived. In the end, she understood, but she was still surprised I had lied to her, even for that. We had grown so close together that she did not believe I would deceive her on purpose.

The moral of the story is, even when we believe it is justified, lying can have a negative effect on our partner. If it is anything other than a wonderful surprise for your partner, never hold back the truth. If your partner feels a surprise is deception, don't do it. I learned a lesson and will never deceive my Sweet Paula again, even if it is to surprise her with something wonderful.

The truth is, I could have told her I had received the money, and the evening would have been just as wonderful but without her feeling deceived.

Men Are Not Mind Readers

Ladies, when you are upset about something, do not expect your man to be able to read your mind or know what is in your heart. Do not blame him if he does not know or notice what your issue is. This is game playing and will lead only to disappointment in you and frustration in your partner. Women have an inherent ability to discern what other people are feeling. Perhaps this is an aspect of their maternal instincts. Men, however, do not have that ability! Women, don't wait for your man to figure it out. Just tell him what's bothering you. He can't do anything if he has no idea what's wrong or what he can do to make it right. Even if you think he should know, most of the time, he doesn't.

Let me make another important point here: If you cut or color your hair, wear a new outfit, change your makeup, paint your fingernails, or move the furniture, do not ask your husband if he notices anything different. The first thing that happens when a man hears those words from his wife is panic. The question itself has just reduced his faculties of logical discernment to mush. You have placed him in a no-win situation, and he knows it. Just tell him. "I colored my hair, what do you think?" or "I bought a new outfit, do you like it?" When you do otherwise, you are setting up you and your husband for disappointment. Men are simply not as discerning as women, and expecting your man to have your instinctual abilities will only end up disappointing you, which men never want to do!

In the same vein, don't wait until an important date has passed and then feel brokenhearted your man forgot. Men can be forgetful; it's just the way we are, especially when we are preoccupied. Give your man hints, clues, and reminders as the date approaches. Don't let him forget, and stop expecting him to think like you do. Here are a few examples.

"Honey, our anniversary is just three months away. Let's go to Jamaica."

"My birthday is next week, and Macy's has a bracelet on sale I absolutely love."

"Honey, Valentine's Day is coming up, and I would like to go out for a special dinner to celebrate our love together. Mind if I make reservations?

Take this same approach for every other day that is important to you. Help your man make you happy! Hat tip to Dr. Laura Schlessinger's *The Proper Care and Feeding of Husbands* for this one. Remember, your man never wants to disappoint you or let you down. Help him to love you better!

Unconditional Love

Everyone needs unconditional love from his or her spouse. This is a decision, not a feeling! How else can we open our hearts and share our deepest secrets? We are not used to unconditional love except (hopefully) from our parents. If you are a Christian, then you understand that God's love for you is unconditional. In fact, God loves us so much that he became a man and then paid the ultimate price for our sins on the cross through his suffering and death. Jesus was willing to show unconditional love by sacrificing his life for us. In the Bible, husbands are commanded show the same sacrificial love to their wives. "Husbands, love your wives, as Christ loved the church and gave Himself up for her" (Ephesians 5:25, AMP).

Regardless of whether or not you are a Christian, your spouse needs unconditional love from you. A wife needs unconditional, *sacrificial,* love from her husband. Yet, the idea goes much further. God's number one commandment is for us to love him, but the second is for us to love each other as we love ourselves.

And you shall love the Lord your God out of and with your whole heart and out of and with all your soul (your life) and out of and with all your mind (with your faculty of thought and your moral understanding) and out of and with all your strength. This is the first and principal commandment. (Deuteronomy 6:4-, 5.)

The second is like it and is this; You shall love your neighbor as yourself. There is no other commandment greater than these. (Mark 12:30–31, AMP)

Is your love for yourself conditional? Of course not. What person does not love him or herself unconditionally? Your spouse needs the security of your unconditional love in order to be happy and to feel secure enough to show his or her true self. Remember, your spouse is a part of you. Love your spouse deeply, and you will find your spouse doing the same for you.

Everyone needs a marriage where his or her partner has agreed to the covenant marriage outlined in this chapter and observes the importance and fulfills the responsibilities of the sacred trust. For real trust between spouses, each one must love the other unconditionally. This will create the foundation for true and lasting intimacy. The first part of achieving intimacy in marriage is to agree to the covenant agreement. Then keep your sacred trust, and build on the foundation of unconditional love for your partner. Remember, unconditional love is a decision, not a feeling!

If you both agree that this is what you believe and want your marriage to be, you have the strong foundation necessary to build a loving, happy, and intimate marriage.

10

PRESERVING OR RESTORING YOUR WIFE'S LOVE AND INTIMACY

I wrote this chapter specifically for husbands, but I expect wives will—and should—read it, too.

Providing his wife has not already left the marriage emotionally, a man has a good chance of turning his marriage around. The trouble is, men do not know when their wife has already checked out emotionally, because wives usually do not reveal this until they are ready for a divorce. A good barometer on this is if she is still making love with you. If lovemaking has stopped, the opportunity to restore the marriage may have passed, but not necessarily. There might still be hope!

The first thing husbands need to understand is that women are the ones with the power, because they are the gatekeepers in the marriage relationship. Therefore, husbands are not in control. You may feel this leaves you at a huge disadvantage. Fortunately, the vast majority of women are eager to have a great marriage with their husband. Women have an inherent need to be loved and adored by their husband. When you start learning to love her how she needs and wants to be loved and become the husband of her dreams, she will respond in ways that will amaze you. The only question is, did you marry a wonderful woman? I am not asking about how she might be today. Did you marry a wonderful woman *originally*? Take a moment and think back to how you felt when you married her. I'm betting your answer is *yes!* Unless she has already left the marriage emotionally, she is still there and wants to be a wonderful wife to you again. You need to believe that in your heart if you are going to have any hope of transforming your marriage.

Depending on how long two people have been married, a husband may have already done a great deal to push his wife away emotionally. This does not mean she hates him, just that she may have a hard time trusting him emotionally. This is because of his part in the downward spiral. It may have started with the decrease in her drive, but most men react and counterpunch emotionally because of their wife's rejection. A good number of those behaviors have probably been negative for her. If you've been married for many years, just look at the number of apologies you have had to issue just to keep life peaceful. Sometimes you may have felt you were in a crisis without any good solutions.

Your wife may have forgiven you, but letting go of the issues that hurt is difficult. This is normal for women and not exclusive to your wife. You need to understand that your wife interprets life through her feelings. She does not approach her feelings with logic like you do. This is not a bad thing when you understand it, because once you do, you can learn how to make her feel wonderful about you! What wife doesn't want to feel like her husband is wonderful?

Unfortunately, she has something hard to deal with that you do not, or at least not to the same degree. Those hurts from the past come back to her repeatedly. Each time a woman is hurt emotionally, the problem compounds itself without you knowing it. Let's take a closer look at this phenomenon so we understand better.

Emotional Replays

Over the years, something about women has amazed me: their tendency to relive the things their man has done to hurt them emotionally. Your wife may bring up something you did from thirty years ago. Remember, women feel things; it's their nature. Your wife may forgive you for doing something, but she is incapable of forgetting it. You may already know this from conversations with your wife. It does not take much for a woman, after being hurt, to start listing the other things you have done to hurt her. You might be shocked, because she is talking about something from the distant past as though it happened yesterday. Old hurts may roll off her tongue as though she has a list all memorized and ready to pound you into the ground.

An emotional replay is when a woman begins to relive hurts from the past as well as the newest one you just caused. The list of hurts rolls off her tongue so easily because of the depth of pain she is feeling from experiencing that past pain all over again. She may have forgiven you for those incidents, but she still feels the pain when she feels unloved by you. In fact, it could even be a hurt caused by someone else, but it compounds your

131

problem and the pain she feels deep within. These are emotional replays, and she can't stop them from happening any more than you can stop from feeling devastated when she refuses your request for lovemaking. You have no control over the depth of pain you experience, and she has no control over experiencing emotional replays.

How do you handle this? The first thing to realize is that women feel better when they are able to express their emotions. Even though she may be criticizing you, you need to let her express her emotions and simply listen. Don't argue, and don't keep apologizing. Just listen, unless she asks for a response. As she expresses herself, try to see the situation from her point of view. Your wife probably had no idea the depth of pain she caused you by refusing your advances. She has no frame of reference for your pain. It is almost impossible for her to understand your reactions and grasp why you did some of the things you did or why you treated her the way you did. When most men don't understand it themselves, they can't possibly explain it to their wives. Your wife still may not know or understand if she has not read this book. She relives these emotional hurts repeatedly. So, here is the first thing you need to learn: In the future, cause as few hurts as possible. You know why you were bitter and treating her the way you did. Since you understand your behavior now, you need to change it permanently!

Three Goals

1. Let It Go

Open your heart and release the pain of her rejection. You know it is not about you personally, even if she thinks it is. Every wife loses desire for her husband and stops wanting him as much. Do you understand that fact? You must think through this and see that it's no one's fault. Think back to that wonderful woman you married. Do you think she ever wanted to hurt you on purpose?

You have probably been told many times that you need to "man up." Well, this is one of those times. If you're feeling hurt, bitter, broken, unloved, or resentful, you cannot do what is needed to turn your marriage around. You have to let it go. You need to have a pivotal moment of truth that will turn the tide for you deep inside. She doesn't know how much she has hurt you or that she is still hurting you. Now that you understand the situation, you need to make changes, but this will not happen if you are walking around hurt and bitter!

2. Love Her Sacrificially

Do you remember courting your wife? The increases you made to her love throttle were so easy for you. Did you make sacrifices to show her you loved her? Do that again. The first thing you need to decide is that you are going to love her with a renewed, sacrificial love, and you are going to pour love into this woman like you have never done in your whole life and in ways you have not even thought of yet. You need to determine you are going to make her love throttle surge forward with your increases, all the way to 110 percent. This is not about kissing up to her; it is about making her feel loved. The number one thing your wife needs from you is love. Are you on board so far?

The next thing you need to realize is this is going to take some time. Have patience, because it will take some effort for you to figure out what is required on your part to transform her back into the woman of your dreams. She will not know what you are doing, but that is your goal.

3. Understand and Accept Reality

No matter what you do, you need to accept that she is not going to transform herself sexually and return to the way she was with you during the sexual peak of your marriage. You will need to accept her wanting to be with you because she loves you and understands your need to feel loved by her. That does not mean she will be with you reluctantly or not enjoy sex with you, it simply means it is not going to be as explosive as it was in the beginning.

Let me ask you a question: If she wants to wrap herself around you because she knows you need her, and she is willing to give herself to you because she loves you and wants to make you happy, is that enough for you? If she is willing to do that as much as you need, then you should accept it with joy! Once the woman of your dreams is wrapping herself around you regularly, your marriage should never experience the downward spiral that has destroyed so many others.

Starting Over

First, you can simply do nothing. You can decide that it is what it is and you are not going to change or do anything differently. Some men find themselves so embittered towards their wife that they make such a decision. Since you are taking the time to read this book, you are educated now about the male and female sex drive. With this knowledge, you should be able to understand why these things have occurred. Until now, you may have made a great effort with little to nothing to show for it. It's time to change that and start getting results.

The things you are going to start doing are not temporary actions designed to get her to change for you or to simply get you sex. Instead, they are changes in lifestyle to help you push and keep pushing her love throttle to over one hundred percent, and the changes need to be permanent! You read about the love actions earlier in the book. Now I will be more specific with the actions and what must be done. I will go into detail so you understand clearly what you need to do.

Create an Environment of Affection

You may recall from the love actions chapter that affection is the action of providing an attitude of love and gentleness in the way you choose to convey yourself to your spouse. Affection sets the tone, atmosphere, and environment for all communication, both verbal and physical, between you and your spouse.

When you were courting, affection for your wife came naturally. You were doing your best to win her

135

heart. Now she might feel you have changed and are not the man she married. The first thing you need to do is get your heart right towards your bride. Forget how bad things are. If you don't start loving this woman with all your heart, there is no chance of happiness with her. This means talking to her and treating her with gentleness and love. You need to start treating her like the princess you met and married.

This must begin by helping her feel like she is living in a home with a husband who is deeply in love with her. Affection will set the tone for communication in your home. You need to take any anger you have and let it go. You will never conquer this woman with anger. It will only cause her to withdraw and not trust in your love. You need to decide to overlook the things she does and says until she sees you are changing and becoming a husband who adores her. Only you can accomplish that. You have to show gentleness in all things. If you provide an atmosphere of love and affection for your wife, you will begin making love throttle increases once again.

A happy marriage does not just happen. Realize your wife has no one to turn to but you to meet her needs. A man will work sixty hours a week, do backbreaking work, get dirty and greasy, come home and mow the lawn and yet, when it comes to meeting his wife's needs, complain about how stupid it is. Do you want a happy life? It won't happen unless you have a happy wife! Trust me; you want her to be as happy and as loved as you can make her feel! Your wife affects your happiness more than you realize. You need to treat her like she is a part of you, because she is. You need to learn her primary love actions, her desires, her method of communicating, and the emotions and thoughts she deals with every day. Once you understand her, you will be able to love her the way she needs to be loved. You will be pushing her love throttle forward!

Sex

For now, other than your normal frequency, do not try to engage in more sex. Your goal is to get her to understand the male reality and start increasing the frequency because she understands you need it. For most women, this is going to take some time, so be patient!

If she comes for a hug, give her a hug. If she wants a kiss, give her a kiss. A hug or a kiss does not mean you should try to bed her unless it is obvious she is inviting it. A woman can easily project sexual desire to her husband if she wants it. This is an area in which you need to exercise some self-control. She needs to be able to hug and kiss you without worrying she will have to disappoint you or reject you. She needs to know you are always there and ready to give her tender touch without any strings attached. More love throttle increases for you! If she feels like she can't come for a hug without you wanting sex, she may not come for them anymore. Let her know you would love to just hug and hold her more without sex. You may need to challenge her so she can see for herself.

Quality Time

As I stated earlier, quality time is time spent together alone without distractions or interruptions. It is time where each spouse is focused solely on the other. Quality time says *you are important to me.* All women who have not already checked out of a marriage emotionally want quality time with their husband. A wife's desire for quality time is an area where men can have little patience and understanding, but women need quality time to feel loved. To a woman, quality time says she is important. How each woman chooses to spend quality time with her husband will vary. Your wife may enjoy sitting on the couch and talking. She might want to walk in the park while holding hands. It could be holding her at night when you go to bed. Every woman wants and needs quality time with her husband.

Use the quality time with her to learn more about what is important to her. Take the opportunity to ask her. Get the number one thing each time and only the number one thing. Then start doing it for her. When she tells you a certain behavior or action is important to her, believe her and do it! Forget the fact it might seem meaningless to you, because she's not you. If you have a list of "honey dos" that you have not completed, get them done.

Make a vow that you will learn how to love her. As you learn to love her the way she needs and wants, you will begin to make real and bountiful increases to her love throttle.

Talking and Listening—Sharing Emotions

Another area where you need to step up is in letting her express her emotions and the things that have happened in her day. This is an important primary love action for women. A woman needs this interaction with her husband. She talks and expresses herself while he listens attentively. Women have an inherent need to express their emotions through conversation. You may have noticed that your wife no longer comes to you and shares anything. If things are that bad between you, you may need to give her a little encouragement to start sharing with you once again. For most women, simply asking how her day went will be enough to get her to begin sharing with you. Keep asking until she starts sharing on her own. Pay particular attention to what she says and her emotions as she expresses herself. It's how these events make her feel that's important. And make sure you don't drift off on her! Not paying attention is rude and sends the message that you don't care about her feelings or what she has to say. Would you have drifted off when you were falling in love with her and wanting her to fall in love with you? No way. Get your heart in the right place, and it will be easy to listen.

Another key point: It's not about *what* happened in her day, but *how she feels* about those things. You might think of it as an opportunity to talk while she sees it as an opportunity to share her feelings with you. I know I am repeating myself, but that's only because I know men can be a little dense in getting this. Appreciate your wife for wanting you to understand her feelings. When you listen to her and understand she is sharing her feelings, you will find yourself getting to know your wife much better and begin understanding what is important to her. When appropriate, empathize with her. This is the perfect time to study her and learn about her. The more you understand her, the easier it will be for you to do the things that are important to her and to make huge love throttle increases.

Cuddling, Snuggling, Hugs, Kisses, and Holding

I talked about this in the sex area, but it is of such importance I am going to expound on it deeper here. Hugs, kisses, cuddling, snuggling, and holding are love actions given mostly by the husband to the wife, and they should occur regularly. If just about every time a husband touches his wife it's a request for sex, she will begin to feel like a sexual object and withdraw from him physically. Men need to realize that women do not feel love through sex and make certain they show their wives a good deal of physical contact apart from their need for sex. Women in general like to cuddle and snuggle if they feel confident it is not going to lead to sex every time.

I know this can be difficult and is asking a great deal from some men. After all, you are already sex-starved, and now I'm saying you can touch, feel, and smell the fruit, but you can't taste it. This is an area where you need to exercise patience and learn new habits. And the changes need to be permanent. If she can get the cuddle or snuggle time she needs just about whenever she wants it, she will be far more likely to do the same for your needs in the bedroom. You may even find you enjoy this time with her.

Acts of Service

Acts of service means doing specific things for your spouse that she will appreciate. Some couples naturally divide some acts of service. One common division is the husband taking out the garbage or mowing the lawn and the wife doing the laundry or dishes. It may or may not include chores. For acts of service to be effective, you need to discuss this with your wife. You want to be certain which acts of service are important to her. Otherwise your actions will be of little to no value. If you pay attention, you can take on some things she may not like to do.

Here is an example: When deciding which act of service to do for my Sweet Paula, I watched her as she did various chores around the house. I noted there was one particular chore (dishes) about which she would procrastinate. Each time it became necessary to do the dishes, she would put it off for as long as possible. It was not hard to see she disdained or even hated it. The truth is, I was not excited about doing the dishes either, but I wanted to find an act of service she would appreciate. Out of sacrificial love, I took that chore and made it mine. I just started doing it. Because she hated doing it so much, she told me she appreciated me for doing it for her. Serious love throttle increases! She lets me know regularly how much she appreciates me doing that chore. Even when she says nothing, I still know I am making increases.

A husband can decide to do a hundred tasks that he thinks are important but which are actually of little value to his wife. Unfortunately, this happens quite often. A husband busts his rear end trying to love his wife yet receives no love throttle increases. Men, you need to get this one. You need to love her with discernment, not just with intensity and sacrifice. Talk to her, observe her, and find out which areas will make a big difference to her. She will appreciate it more than you know.

Every week or two, ask her for something, anything that you can do to make her happier. Then implement the change. Don't grab a list of fifteen right off the bat. If she has several items, start with the one that is most important to her, and then add the next most important thing on her list the following week and so on. If you try to do everything at once, she won't appreciate it nearly as much, and it could lead to a complete failure on your part to do any of it. Plus, you do not want to come across as doing things out of desperation but out of a heartfelt and genuine love for her. Keep it up, and the day will come when she will tell you that you already do everything she could ever ask. That is the day you will know you have accomplished the major change you were after in your efforts to make her happy. She will know it, too! Her engine will be running hard, and the two of you will be growing in intimacy.

Words of Praise

How this looks will be different for everyone, but you need to speak words of praise to her and about her every day. You can speak of her intelligence, beauty, maturity, wisdom, common sense, insightfulness, kindness, honesty, tenderness, intuition, talent, and so on. This is very important and makes huge love throttle increases. If you can't find wonderful things to say about your spouse, both to her and to others, you have a serious problem, and I would question whether your love for her is genuine!

Your wife needs this from you far more than you may realize. Do not make things up or be insincere in any way. Women have a built-in BS (bologna/salami) detector when it comes to their husbands, and making things up to score points will not make love throttle increases. Your compliments need to be sincere in every way!

Touch

If one of your wife's primary love action needs is touch, then you need to make sure you are giving her regular physical affection without it leading to sex. This includes hugs, kisses, handholding, rubbing, brushing, and touching her regularly. Always take the time to hold her for a while after sex. Although this is true of most women, it is particularly important when touch is a woman's primary love action.

People who need touch require it to feel loved by their spouse. Although I have seen this as more of a male need, it is also a need for many women and will make huge love throttle increases when you do it without any conditions or expectations.

Talking with Her

Your wife is not stupid; she is going to see the changes you are making on her behalf. At first, she may be suspicious and wonder what you want or what you are up to. Don't worry about it. You probably had that trial when you first met her, too. Just keep showing her how much you love her. Eventually, she will wonder what has happened to you. When that conversation happens, be ready!

Trust me when I tell you she will see the change in you and be grateful for it. Some men will begin to experience more intimacy with their wife soon; others will take more time. Your wife needs to see it is not just a tactic or a phase you are going through. After you have proven the change is real and you're not going to revert back to your old self, it's time to explain why you changed.

Before you do that, I recommend you make a list of things you want to discuss with her. Some items will be unique to your relationship, but others need to be the things you have learned about the downward spiral in marriage. Do not attempt to talk to her without an organized list of things you want her to understand. When men get emotional, they have a tendency to forget important details.

Also, I have emphasized the need to use the love actions, but the biggest change on your part is adopting an affectionate, loving attitude and a forgiving heart. Once you forgive her, even though it was not her fault, you can move on to dealing with and changing your heart attitude towards her. It is my sincere belief that your realization of the truth about marriage and what happens will help you to start being the man of her dreams once again, showing your love through the love actions you have learned. Win her back! You won her heart once, so you can do it again. Enjoy sweeping this woman off her feet once more.

When she comes to talk, don't just blurt stuff out. If she is eager, let her know it is so important you want to have the time to work out how to clearly express what is happening to you. Plan an evening when you will have some quality time together. Maybe you can take her for a romantic dinner first. A loving card is always good. Let her see the man she fell in love with is back again. Then, whether it is a walk in the park or just time sitting together, explain what you have learned. Apologize for the things you have done to hurt her! Tell her how you never want to hurt her again and promise you won't. Tell her how much you love her and want an intimate relationship with her. Express to her how you feel about her and the depth of your love for her.

Explain what you learned from the book about women's and men's sex drives and how you want to restore your romance and love together. Explain from your heart how you felt when she rejected you and that you did not understand it yourself, hence there was little to no hope of you being able to explain it to her. Offer to read the book together with her and discuss it in detail. This is when you need to help her understand the truth about men. Explain sexual intercourse and how having her wrapped lovingly around you is the primary way you receive feelings of love from her. Let her know that although there is a physical aspect to it, the primary thing you receive from her through intercourse is love and intimacy. Tell her that you need that feeling of love from her to be happy. Help your wife understand this is the main way every husband receives love from his wife.

Encourage her to read this book so she can gain a better understanding of everything you've learned. Tell her you do not need fireworks in the bedroom every time, just her sincere desire to be with you because she understands your needs and loves you enough to meet them.

Allow your wife time to digest all the new information and realize her dream man is back. In the beginning, some wives may be cynical or skeptical that the transformation is real or that it will last. This is where time is your friend. Because with your new understanding, in time she will see your change is genuine. Just keep pushing her throttle forward. Never stop being creative in finding ways to be romantic and show her you love her. Stay the course, and you will find your wife wants to be a wonderful wife to you as well. Your engines will run high, and your marriage will soar to a new level of wonderful intimacy together.

You are not Casanova

Every man likes to believe he is a good lover. It's a macho thing. The truth is, unless a man has been educated about lovemaking and female orgasms, he's probably not a good lover. Few natural talents are going to pop through and make her feel like you are Superman.

Did you know many women sneak orgasms and don't tell their partner? Do you know why? When a woman is driving toward an orgasm and she tells her man she is going to finish, what should he do? Most men react instinctively by increasing speed or thrust. If they're having oral sex, he may increase intensity. He may even say something sexy to try to encourage her. All of these things can actually prevent her from having an orgasm. Just when she was about to reach orgasm, he yanks it away from her!

Here's a tip: If your woman tells you she is about to finish, just keep doing what you're doing. Whatever you were doing brought her to that point, so don't change anything!

Becoming a great lover is a learned behavior, and most wives are not capable of teaching you, although your wife can give you some instructions about herself. This is an area you need to research, because there is a lot of wonderful material out there. If you want her to make love with you more often, you need to learn to be a great lover.

Here's one final tip: After you've climaxed, do not just turn over and go to sleep. Hold her and love on her for a while. Show her your appreciation for her taking care of you. The one exception is if you have a strong need for touch. In this case she may already receive enough touch from you and this may not be as important to her. These two tips are minor, but if you err on either one, it will make a big difference to her.

What if She's Having an Affair?

If you discover your wife is having an affair, your options may be limited. First, you need to decide if you want to stay married to her. If you decide you want to make the marriage work, you might have an uphill battle that is going to be difficult for you. Most likely, she has experienced sex with him that is beyond anything you are capable of making her feel. That said, it does not mean you cannot win her back. If you have a church, get your pastor involved!

The first thing you need to do is insist the affair end immediately. Force her to make a choice. She may want time, but time is not going to help a woman in limbo. She has not made a decision this entire time on whether she wants you or him. The best chance for you to get her back is to stand up as a man and force her to make a decision. Don't be a wimp! Women don't respect weak men.

Explain what you've learned from this book about the three enigmas and the downward spiral in marriage. Explain that you understand how she may feel and how she may believe sex with the new man is out of this world. Show her from this book how it's like that for all women in an affair but that it's doomed to fail. Explain that she will have the same problem again, and all she is accomplishing is hurting people. Ask her if she is ready to tell everyone she has left you for another man. Her response will be a key factor in determining where she is emotionally.

If your wife decides to stay with you, then you will need all the information on the other man. Who is he? Where do they meet? How do they communicate? If it is someone she works with, she will need to find another job.

If she decides to stay with you, it may take some time to get her head around what you have learned and believe you are going to love her regardless of what she has done. I suggest lots of quality time together and that you begin making huge increases in her love throttle. She most likely got into the affair because she felt abandoned emotionally and was lonely. Don't ever let her feel that way again.

11

PRESERVING OR RESTORING YOUR HUSBAND'S LOVE AND INTIMACY

Today, wives are brainwashed in a culture of liberalism and feminism. Even wives who reject these beliefs are bombarded daily with feminist messages about women and men. I don't mean messages about equal rights for women or equal pay for an equal job; almost everyone agrees with that. I'm talking about messages that tell us men are dumb, selfish brutes.

Sitcom after sitcom portrays men as complete fools and women as the ones who encompass great wisdom and intelligence. Women may believe they are able to separate fantasy from reality, but far more of this messaging gets absorbed than they realize.

Are we to believe that women with mostly secular liberal backgrounds have discovered the keys to happiness in marriage? None that I've heard! Does anyone believe that only women are the wise ones with superior knowledge and wisdom? Let me surprise you by saying that in some areas, women certainly are, but in other areas, it is the man. In truth there's a balance. No man is an island of happiness and knowledge, and neither is any woman.

The key is to understand and embrace our distinctive roles as women and men. It is about how to love each other in a way that brings true joy, happiness, and wonderful intimacy. Couples need to embrace and then act on each other's wants and needs. That said, our culture has given women the keys to marriage. If you are a woman, you are in control of your marriage. I'm not saying women can do anything and get the results they want. Rather, women have the have the ability to transform their marriage. Husbands can only do so by persuading their wife it is in her best interest. Wives, however, can simply begin making the needed changes.

Women can either embrace liberal feminism in their marriage or embrace genuine happiness. The two are contrary to each other when it comes to love and intimacy. I know women who hold feminist views of marriage, and not a single one has an intimate marriage with a genuinely happy husband. Trust me when I say that if a husband is not happy with his wife, he will not be too concerned with making her happy either. Marriage is mutual, and neither spouse is superior to the other.

Another extreme is men who think they can rule over their wife and marriage. Any man who believes he can rule over his wife and be happy is clueless. He might control her to a degree, but she will not be happy, and neither will he.

Marriage is not about whom is in charge or who is more intelligent. Each spouse has strengths and weaknesses. It has everything to do with understanding and then loving your spouse and pushing his or her love throttle to over one hundred percent. A spouse whose love throttle is over one hundred percent will be eager to do just about anything, within reason, to make his or her partner happy and feel loved. Do you want a partner who does what you want grudgingly after your continual nagging and complaining, or do you want a partner who is looking constantly for new ways to love you and please you? These are polar opposites, and so too are people who control their partner and the people who love them. Which do you want to be?

Men and Emotions

Unfortunately, men are not great at assessing their emotions. Men need time to consider what they are feeling. If a man is experiencing feelings he has never experienced before, he may have a much harder time dealing with them in his logical mind. What is he feeling? Why is he feeling it? Should he feel it? What can he do about it? Women are just the opposite. They know almost immediately what they are feeling and can express it easily. Women have never been told they are not entitled to their feelings, whereas men are told to "suck it up" or "man up." For a man, showing emotions is often considered a sign of weakness.

Because of the way men are with their emotions, when new emotions pop up, they are ill-suited to handle them. First, the man has to identify what he is feeling. Then he needs to figure out why he is feeling it. Is it legitimate to feel the way he does? Can he do anything about the situation?

151

The cold, hard truth is that until we fell in love, it would have been impossible for any woman to make us feel the way our wife makes us feel. Until we are married, we do not expect our woman to make love to us. Although we realize there may be times when she says no, we are totally unprepared for the frequency of rejection we are about to experience. Furthermore, we have no idea of the emotional impact this is going to have on us.

To illustrate this, I'm going to tell you a short story about a couple I counseled. Unfortunately, this story is too common in marriage.

Roger & Mary

Roger and Mary came to see me about some problems they were having. Their problems seemed solvable if the two were willing to compromise in a few areas, so I knew there was more to this than they were telling me.

I inquired about their love life. Mary told me they did not have much of one, that sex was not important for either one of them. Roger just sat there silently. After counseling many men, I knew this could not possibly be true, so I asked Roger straight out if he wished they had more sex.

"Of course I do," Roger replied, "but that's okay."

I explained to Roger and Mary about the male need for sex to feel loved by his wife and how emotionally devastating it was for Roger to be rejected. Mary assured me that was not the case with Roger. So I turned to Roger

---

and asked Roger if he felt rejected and hurt when Mary refused his advances.

"Yes." he replied, "but I don't understand why."

"In fact, doesn't it break your heart and devastate you emotionally that Mary says no so often?"

Tears began streaming down Roger's face. He couldn't speak as he fought back his emotions, but he nodded. Mary was shocked by Roger's answer and the overwhelming emotions that were breaking through. She had no idea Roger was holding in such deep emotions about sex.

The truth is, Roger didn't understand what he was feeling until I spoke openly about it. He had just locked away his feelings, figuring he had no right to feel how he did. Men are supposed to be macho after all, not wimpy or heart-wrenched babies.

Different men will handle their wife's rejection differently, but all will be devastated emotionally if they genuinely love their wife. Show me a man who is not heartbroken by rejection, and I'll show you a man with either a serious problem or a man who is not in love with his wife. The lone exception is the husband with a lover.

Every man deals with rejection in a different way. We have no frame of reference or way to categorize or understand what we are feeling or why we are feeling it. We are slow to understand emotions anyway, and often we think it's just sex and our emotions are not valid. The truth is, for a man in love, sex is the gateway to his heart. If you want to get your man to open up and share his desires and secrets, the bedroom is the place to start. This is where you can find the little boy who adores you.

Mothers

A phenomenon for men raised in our culture is a mother who was a dominant figure in his life. She was the one who taught him how to love, and he learned that she would love him unconditionally no matter what he did. A man raised in such an environment loved and adored his mother unconditionally. Yet, when she was disappointed in him, he may have felt shame and failure that he let her down after trying so hard to make her proud. When a man takes a wife, to a degree, she takes on the same role as his mother. This is true whether we admit it or not. As men, one of the last things we want is to let our wife down or have our wife disappointed in us. This unconditional love for our mother transferred to our wife, and I believe it is the biggest reason why most men do not want a divorce. Of course child welfare, child custody, and finances are also strong incentives for a man to stay married.

This puts the relationship out of balance to a degree and causes us to search harder, whether or not we are right in what we do or the way we feel. We are used to a woman instructing us on what is right and wrong and how we should feel. So, when our wife tells us we should not be upset because it is "just sex," her opinion sinks in hard and deep. We want to take that instruction and process it as true. There's just one problem: She's wrong! This confuses the man further and can complicate his feelings about the matter. She has told him he should not get upset when told no, so he represses his feelings, or at least he attempts to. The truth is he must hide what he is feeling, because she has told him he is not justified in feeling hurt and rejected. He may refuse to deal with his feelings, but in time, his resentment will grow. Eventually, he will lash out in some form, and his actions will not be healthy for the marriage.

Respect

Apart from sex, one of the key things a man needs from his wife is for her to show him respect. Respect is a deep feeling of admiration for someone elicited by his or her abilities, qualities, or achievements. Men need their wife to feel this way about them and express these feelings regularly in order to feel loved.

Men equate love and respect. A man cannot love a woman he does not respect. In fact, the more respect he has for her, the more he will love her. This is important, because if he believes his wife does not respect him, he will also believe she could not possibly love him. A husband may do and say many things to hurt his wife, but he will not show her disrespect. This is because he could not love a woman if he did not respect her. If your man is showing disrespect, he is likely in self-preservation mode!

When you refuse your husband's request for sex, he also feels disrespected. You have shown little regard for his strong need to have you, and this causes him to feel unloved by you. This simple male logic may help you understand why your rejection is so devastating for him. It will cause major decreases to his love throttle every time. Some women may have a hard time accepting these truths about men. If you are in this category, I encourage you to do a little survey of men and ask them about the relationship between love and respect.

Why The Wives?

Wives might be wondering why I have written this book more towards them. The answer should be obvious by now: Wives, not husbands, are the gatekeepers to sex. In modern culture, women hold the power. Women are the ones who change first and whose drive begins to fall. Women are the ones who limit their husband's access to them, and they were the first person to make substantial decreases to their spouse's love throttle. It is women who begin the pattern of sexual denial, sometimes not understanding why. Plus, women read more than men, and my hope is they will begin understanding their husbands and restore love and intimacy in their marriages.

Women in feminized modern culture have been taught that everything is about them and their happiness. All of society tells them they have every right to be selfish and think just of themselves in these matters. Men do not matter. If women don't want to do it, they shouldn't have to do it. After all, we are not living in caveman days anymore. Women are free and liberated. They do not have to do it just for him! Perhaps, but ask yourself: Why do you think seventy-two percent of men cheat on their wives and seventy percent of women cheat on their husbands? Can even one woman say it's because she and her husband have too much sex? Without a doubt, it's the enigmas we have identified that are wreaking havoc on marriages!

Do you want a kind, loving, affectionate, and considerate husband? Then meet his needs, and you will have a husband who will move the planet to make you happy. A happy man will live to make his wife happy; it will be his primary goal in life. He will love her, support her, adore her, think she is the best woman in the whole world, and he will make sure everyone he knows hears it. I understand he may not be meeting all of your needs, but I will discuss that in a bit.

Your husband needs you so badly it drives him crazy! He has no control over being a man, and this is the primary way men feel loved by their wives. This is the first thing you need to realize. Do you want to be married or would you rather live the life of a spinster? Most women need their husband just as badly as he needs her, just in different ways. If your husband loves you and bends over backwards to make you happy, isn't it worth it to meet his needs and make him happy, too?

In *The Proper Care and Feeding of Husbands,* Dr. Laura tells women if they will just make love with their husband, they will almost always enjoy it themselves. Here is an excerpt from her book, in which she is having a conversation with a caller:

> "I then went on to ask her about the times she
> "didn't feel like it" but did it anyway:

DR. LAURA: Didn't you get turned on at some point in the lovemaking?

CALLER: (giggling) Yes.

DR. LAURA: Well then, sometimes the pump just needs a little priming.... And didn't you feel great about him and life in general after a good orgasm?

CALLER: (giggling again) Yes.[18]

My Sweet Paula says many times she is not in the mood at all, but she goes forward with lovemaking in a spirit of genuine love and affection towards me, because she understands my needs. Yet, after starting, she finds it stimulates her. She says it always ends up being enjoyable even though she was not in the mood. She begins doing it out of love and respect because she understands men but says her engine always gets going after a while. Women almost universally report having this same response. Since this is the case with most women, wives need to take care of their husband's needs out of a deep and genuine love.

Here is an article from the Huffington Post written by one wife (Megan Conly) who realized her drive had fallen and decided to take some action. Its title is "5 Reasons To Have Sex With Your Husband." Here is just a part of her piece. I want you to see what she reported when she decided to change things:

Ibid, pp.133–134.

2. If you want your husband to act like a man, you need to treat him like a man. Hold the eye rolls. I am not pushing for a return to the 1950's. (Although, heaven knows an era in which low rise jeans did not exist is basically alright by me.) Women need any number of criteria met to feel loved. Men are far simpler. They need to be fed, they need to be appreciated, and they need to have sex. That is it. Really. So make or order dinner once in a while. Say thank you for the long hours spent at work with a hug and smile when he walks through the door each night. (Better yet? Smile as you hand him the kids and walk out the door for a long, much needed break.) And my goodness, let the poor man see you naked. It is astounding what a good man will do for a good woman that has made him feel loved. After a few weeks of meals and make outs, you will sit back and wonder why you didn't insist on having sex every night sooner. Talk about a small investment and big returns.

3. You need to have a moment in each day that is just about the two of you. Remember that boy? The one that made your heart thump and hands sweat? The one that called when you hoped he would, that made you run hot and high up to the stars until you thought you would never come down? He is still there. Under the years and bills and

worries, that smiling boy is still in love with and needs his smiling girl. Every night after the kids go to bed is a chance to find him again. A moment to remind yourself that you are living a picket fenced adventure and my goodness, there is nothing the two of you can't do.[19]

Since so many women report great results, why not give it a try? What do you have to lose? Plus, remember that when two people enter into a marriage covenant, they are committing to a sacred trust. They are trusting that their most personal desires and needs will be met exclusively by their marriage partner. Implicit in this agreement is that each spouse will willingly and lovingly meet all of his or her partner's needs. This is not something to take lightly. This is a solemn responsibility! Sex is not optional or just something you do when you're in the mood. Your partner has entered into a sacred trust with you, to allow you and you alone to meet those needs. Once you understand what those needs are, it is your responsibility to meet them if you want a happy and intimate marriage. Once again, the rewards far outweigh the sacrifice when you find your heart's desires and needs being met as well.

As Dr. Laura goes on to say in her book, (I paraphrase) a wife will change dirty diapers, clean poop

---

[19] Meg Conley (November 6, 2014). "Five Reasons Why You Should Have Sex With Your Husband Every Night." HuffingtonPost.com, accessed March 9, 2016, http://www.huffingtonpost.com/meg-conley/five-reasons-you-should-h_b_5647291.html 2016

and vomit from floors and blankets, wash dishes, cabinets, counters, do laundry, scrub and vacuum the floors, hold a crying baby for hours when it is sick, walk the dog, and pick up his poop. Yet, she will draw a line in the sand when it comes to meeting her husband's sexual needs. This is pure, self-defeating selfishness, and it breaks her husband's heart and spirit. His withdrawal for self-protection will be uncontrollable and will cause him to be far less willing to give her what she needs from him.

Sometimes neither partner understands what his or her partner's needs are. However, once understood, both partners need to realize the sacred trust they have to meet each other's needs. If either person is unwilling to take care of the covenant partner, they should not have gotten married! As covenant partners, we are responsible to make certain we meet each other's needs. If not, it should come as no surprise when our partner gets those needs met elsewhere, which happens seventy-two percent of the time! If you want a marriage with wonderful intimacy, you must create a loving environment by fulfilling your spouse's needs and doing your part in the sacred trust to prevent any more downward spirals.

A wife who gives herself to her husband with a reluctant spirit is wasting her time. It's not just sex. He needs you to want to be with him. Please understand this! A husband can accept his wife making love because she loves him and she knows he needs her so long as she wraps herself around him and shows her love for him in the process. It will not meet his needs if she gives it to him with no feeling or out of a sense of obligation. That

161

is a waste of time for both people. If what most women believed was true, that it was "just sex," then her expressing an attitude of love would not matter. Yet, it makes all the difference in the world. A man cannot feel loved through the process if his wife is not doing it in a spirit of genuine love or desire.

You may feel like you have a long list of issues or ways you desire to be loved. The best time in the world to talk to your husband and get great results is when he feels loved by you. When do you think that might be? Yes, after making love with him. But do not come to him with a long list of issues to clobber the poor soul. You do not want to give the impression you are giving sex to get things from him. Instead, use the time to explain what you have learned about men and that you will be meeting his needs from now on. It may take some time for him to believe you, but the proof is in the pudding. If lovemaking becomes regular, he will know you mean it.

Use your quality time to share with him things you need from him or ways you need him to show love to you. Ask for one item every week or two. Also, ask him what you can do to show him your love for him. Find out what other love actions are important to him. Sex might be number one, but there's a number two and three. For example, most men need their wife to spend recreational time with them. They also need praise and respect. Both husband and wife need to learn how the other needs to be loved and then pour his or her whole heart into the other. Push each other's love throttle to over one hundred percent.

Cut The Attitude

Wives also need to provide an atmosphere of affection toward their husband. Many women become like a parent at times and speak to their husbands with a curt attitude. They talk down to him and are disrespectful. You may get the results at the moment, but when a woman does this, she is making serious decreases to his love throttle. Speaking to your man in terse tones will not make him feel loved, but controlled or at minimum like he let you down. Regardless, it is not positive and makes love throttle decreases.

Every man knows that if his wife is upset with him, she will not make love with him. Some women use this to keep a distance between herself and her husband. She will take something she can let go of and hold onto it, because she knows he knows not to come for sex when she is upset. This is game playing and makes serious decreases on his love throttle. You need to start realizing how important you are to him and how much he needs to be with you. Notice I said *"needs* to be with you" not *"wants* to be with you."

A Cheerful Giver

The Bible tells us that God loves a cheerful giver (2 Corinthians 9:7). If you give your money out of obligation, it means little to God. God wants you to give him your tithe because you love him, not because you are expected to do it. It's the same with your husband and sex. When your husband realizes you are willing to give him sex when he needs it, he may test you. After all, you've had complete control. Now you are relinquishing that control, at least partially, to him. You need to make certain you are expressing an attitude of love towards him when he approaches you and then do your best to enjoy the time with him.

In the previous chapter, I covered in detail how to learn about your partner, so I am not going to repeat every word here. Generally speaking, the principles aren't much different. Learn the things that are important to him and then do them. His happiness is not just about sex. It's just that sex has been the stumbling block for most couples and the primary reason for their downward spiral. You need to learn how to make significant increases in other ways as well to have a happy and intimate marriage.

Your Appearance

Here is an area that, because of a lack of understanding, often makes women feel their husband is shallow. Women seem to be under an illusion about their husband's happiness and love when it comes to the way their husband responds to major changes they make to their appearance. For some reason, women lose their minds and believe that regardless of whatever changes they make, their husbands should be fine with it and continue to believe they are beautiful. In truth, sometimes the changes are revolting to him. This is akin to throwing tempered glass on a concrete floor as hard as you can and believing the glass should not shatter into a thousand pieces just because it was tempered.

Men are geared towards a visual response; it is how we are wired. It's in our DNA, and there's nothing any man can do to change that about himself. Women need to take some time, think about it, and get this one! Just as I told the men earlier about understanding a woman's need to be able to hug and kiss without fear it will lead to sex, this is an area where women need to stop, take a breath, and then take it in and understand it. Men are visually-oriented creatures. If he does not feel some physical attraction to you, there will be no chemistry, and he will never fall—or stay—in love.

Even so, after marriage, many women make major changes to their appearance without regard for the way their husband feels. Somehow these women conjure up in their mind that if he loves her, he should be fine with whatever she wants to do. A woman who thinks this is clueless about men.

A fast way to make deep and steady decreases to his love throttle is to take this attitude, which is selfish and disrespectful and shows you are callous about his feelings. A woman may believe that what she has done is just as pretty as or even prettier than before, but if her man believes it is a major change for the worse, look out! There will always be a huge love throttle price to pay for this selfishness. The woman can think all she wants about it being her body and her right to do what she wants, but we are not talking about legal rights. We are talking about intimacy and love and happiness together. We are talking about making as many love throttle increases and as few decreases as possible.

Remember when I told you about how boys grow up dreaming about marrying a beautiful woman and making love to her? That beauty is in the eyes of the beholder, her husband. This is an area so serious that refusing to take his feelings into consideration when making major changes to your appearance can have serious results much deeper than most women realize. He could find the changes so revolting that you might as well just spit into his face ten times a day, because to him, that's essentially what you're doing. Are you grasping the seriousness of this issue?

Let's get some perspective here. All men realize their sweetheart is going to age. I have never heard a man complain his wife looks too old. Aging is a normal part of life, and none of us can control it. Just about every man adores his wife as she ages. Most women's bodies also change after childbirth, which is also normal, and we understand there may be little our wife can do about it. I point these things out, because women need to understand it is not simply about the way she looks but *why* she looks that way. A wife may get cancer and all of her hair may fall out, but her husband will love and adore her just the same. I am not speaking of normal life and things a woman cannot control.

Four areas of female appearance are of extreme importance to most men yet controlled almost exclusively by women: 1) what she wears, 2) how much she weighs, 3) the length, color, and style of her hair, and 4) and her make-up/perfume. A major change to any of these four areas can send your husband into a tailspin that can make major decreases to his love throttle and have long-lasting negative effects. Women may falsely believe their husband will adjust or get used to it, but trust me when I tell you that he won't! He may stop saying anything, but something that's of major importance to a man is the way his wife looks. Every time you are in his sight, he beholds his beautiful woman. To make changes that cause him to stop seeing you that way is incredibly destructive and self-defeating.

Several times a wife has appeared in my office to talk about how her husband is like a stranger to her. She tells me she is lonely and wants her man to spend time with her and be with her. She will complain he no longer desires her anymore. He is often curt and short when speaking with her. She will complain he no longer has much regard for how she is feeling. He wants to spend time with everyone else or do anything but spend time with her.

When her husband comes in to talk, a common theme emerges. She has made major changes to her appearance that he finds repulsive. Some husbands say they barely recognize their wife anymore. In each case, the woman has made a major change in one of the four areas I listed. Each time it was without consulting her husband, and each time she blamed him for not accepting the changes she made. "If he loved me," the wife says, "these changes wouldn't matter." That is complete nonsense. So, let me make this clear: Your husband cannot control this even if he wanted to. It is the way men are wired.

Double Whammy

In some cases, not only has the wife made changes that he finds repulsive, by doing so in spite of or regardless of his feelings, she has humiliated him by showing great disrespect. Remember, respect is a primary need for a husband to feel loved. Now the wife has said his feelings in this area are of no importance to her. So, not only has she made changes he finds repulsive, she has added disrespect to the mix. It's not that she did something disrespectful and he needs to let it go. She has done and continues to be in his face doing something disrespectful to him. It's the constant state of her appearance.

The degree to which a husband will react depends on the degree of change his wife has made. Every time she refuses to consider his feelings when making changes to her appearance, she makes a significant negative push on his love throttle. If the changes she has made take time to correct, the deep hurt will only heal when she is back to her original appearance, or at least close to it. If she realizes the gravity of this and apologizes, she should also take extra actions to make significant love throttle increases to reestablish her sincere and deep love for him. This will take time and effort on her part, because what she has done is far more serious than she believed.

If you want to make changes, consult with him first! Don't change anything major unless he agrees. Then, even if the changes end up being something he hates, there's no disrespect on top of the changes so he will not feel unloved by you.

Dressing or Looking Dowdy

Too many women refuse to fix themselves up daily or wear horrible-looking clothing to bed. They wear clothing that their husband finds unattractive or don't bother to fix their hair or put on makeup. Each time he sees her, she looks anything but attractive. This tells her husband that his wife doesn't care whether he finds her attractive or not. This is disrespectful at best. Why would any women want most other women to look better to her husband than her? Does this make any sense at all, especially with such horrible cheating statistics? Women need to think hard about this one. This sort of behavior is like asking your husband to see most other women as more beautiful than you.

This is a simple problem to avoid. Why create a monster in your marriage out of selfishness or laziness? Women need to understand their husband is a visual creature and do their best to keep him dreaming about how beautiful she is.

Common Refrains About Sex by Women

"I don't feel up to it."

Are there times when it's okay to say *no* to your husband? Of course! If you are genuinely ill, just about every man who loves his wife will understand and will not want to impose himself on her. Problems arise because many women use every excuse in the book to get out of lovemaking with their husband. Then, when she really is sick, he either doesn't believe her, or he has no sympathy for her, because she has played the card so often. Make sure that when you tell your man no because you're sick, you really are sick.

Women may ask, "But what if my day has been frustrating or I am just not feeling that great or I'm feeling exhausted?" I'm sorry, but those are not good reasons to make your husband feel unloved, rejected, and heartbroken. How about making love to your husband so you both feel better? Just let him know you need a little extra spoiling.

While writing this book, I came across some YouTube videos by Dr. Laura that I think can help women understand this better, because it comes from a woman's perspective. Here is the link to one of them: https://www.youtube.com/watch?v=h-RAmOduAiA. Copy and paste this into any browser, or search YouTube for "Saying No to Your Husband's Advances." This is the only place I've seen where a woman gets it and understands men. Dr. Laura, by the way, has the best insight into men of any author I have ever read. If you want to understand men better, I highly recommend you read her book, *The Proper Care and Feeding of Husbands*.

"My husband is oversexed!"

This is a common refrain from women. How do you know he is oversexed? What is your measure or standard? Many women ask their female friends how often they have sex with their husbands, hoping to get some idea of what's normal. The problem is; they are asking a woman whose drive for her own husband is most likely down a great deal and whose marriage has also suffered many downward spirals. As a result, most wives believe their husbands are oversexed.

Why would you think your man is oversexed any more than the next man? More importantly, what difference does it make what your friend's husband's sex drive is? Are you going to try and regulate your husband based on something you heard from someone else about her husband's drive instead of what your own husband needs? What kind of sense does that make?

One time I was talking with a wife who told me if she let her husband have her as much as he wanted, he would take her ten times a day. Well, she may believe that, but there is almost no man who can have ten orgasms from the time he wakes up until he goes to sleep. If she is referring to a twenty-four-hour period of time, then yes, that is possible, but not daily, as she proclaimed.

Your husband might be able to do it five times a day for a few days in a row or maybe occasionally, but he can't do that every day. That often happens when a man is starving for his wife, and she lets him take all he wants. This is more like bringing a kid into the ice cream shop who has not been allowed ice cream for a long time and telling him he can have as much as he wants. The kid will most likely eat himself full of ice cream. Take the same kid and let him have ice cream every day. Most likely, on some days he will not even care about ice cream. Regardless, if a man needs his wife, he needs her!

Most women are far more likely to be faced with a man who desires her from once every two or three days, to one to three times a day. Some of this can be dependent on the man's age. If a man does not desire his wife almost daily, there is a problem, and she needs to get to the bottom of it! Right now, you may be saying to yourself, *every day?* Yes, it is possible that he may need you every day. Think about it: Is he going to love you any less on one day than another? Remember, for him, sex is the most important way he feels love from you. Once again, I would like to refer you to a You-Tube video by Dr. Laura that I came across while doing research for this book. She is straightforward about men, wives, and sex. Please take the time to watch it. Here is the link: https://www.youtube.com/watch?v=S4VTG9R_lZA. You may also search YouTube for: "He wants it all the time, I don't." Women need to engage their husbands and make the most of it by enjoying the encounter.

"I'm too busy for sex"

Many women have filled their schedules so full that they have little or no time for making love. Women feel their husband should understand how overwhelmed they are with all of the things they have to do and give them a break. If this is your situation, you need to change your schedule! How do you think it makes your husband feel to see he is the last item you intend on taking care of and that you may not get to him? Seriously? No time for him? Why would any man want to be married to you, or, for that matter, any woman who puts him last in her life? No man would! You are pulling back on his love throttle in so many areas at once that your marriage is going to be in a free fall, if it isn't already.

If a woman finds she is too busy for her husband, she shouldn't be surprised when he leaves her for another woman who does have time for him. Talk about being disrespectful and downright mean. Why did this woman marry this man? I'm sorry, but as a man, this one is a crash and burn excuse. Any woman who finds herself in this situation has probably done it on purpose to avoid spending time with her husband. The truth is, "busy" is just an excuse, not a reason. Better to just say the obvious: "I don't want to be with you!"

Once again, Dr. Laura addresses this subject from the view of a woman, so as a man, I will defer to her. Here is the link:

https://www.youtube.com/watch?v=JkAkEVRW5pY.

"I'm not in the mood."

This is an excuse many married men hear often from their wife. This is a major problem in modern culture where women believe that everything in life is all about how they feel. Such women have little to no regard for their husband, because it is all about how she feels and what she wants.

What if a husband were to take the same attitude and simply quit his job because he did not feel like working anymore? Why should he have to do something he doesn't feel like doing? What if he doesn't feel like putting up with that attitude but he does feel like getting a girlfriend? Is that okay? Does this break the covenant agreement any more than the wife refusing to fulfill her marital responsibilities, because she doesn't feel like it?

A man's bitterness towards his wife for this excuse can be so overwhelming that he may feel justified in getting a lover on the side. What are his alternatives? Turn to porn? We are looking at statistics of seventy-two percent of men cheating. I would conclude that a man in this situation is closer to ninety-five percent chance of cheating. Once again, Dr. Laura speaks to this: https://www.youtube.com/watch?v=da9qpmU2vTA

In truth, how a husband or wife feels should have little to nothing to do with them keeping their sacred trust to fulfill each other's needs.

The Husband's Drive to Make His Wife Happy

When a wife takes care of her husband and meets his needs and desires, she will find she has a man who wants to give her the universe. I believe this resonates from childhood and wanting to please our mothers. We always wanted to make her happy and make her proud of us. Now our wife is the woman whom we have chosen, and we want to dedicate our life to making her happy. Yes, I said, *dedicate our life to making her happy!* Some women are amazed that this could be the case given the current state of their husband's behavior and what they have experienced with their husband, but do you remember how he treated you during courtship?

Many men are so consumed with wondering whether they will get to have their wife that day, that sex becomes an obsession. Any time his mind is not consumed with business, he is wondering if today might be a day she lets him have her. If he knows with certainty he cannot have her, he will be feeling bitter towards her. Unfortunately, this husband is not about to move heaven and Earth for his wife, because he cannot get past the fact he is starving for her. His mind is fastened on when she will let him have her, so he never has the opportunity to sit back and be a good husband. You may be wondering if this can be true. Trust me, it is!

Let's take the same husband and give him all the sex he needs and meet his heart's desires. What will he be thinking about when he's not busy? Any clue, women? He will be thinking about how much he loves his wife. He will feel like he is married to the most wonderful woman he knows and be pondering what he can do to make her happier. His mind will be free to be creative and romantic towards her as well. This wife will find she is married to a man who is completely different from the sex-starved man she used to know. This man will want to provide an atmosphere of love and affection for his wife, especially if he believes this is the way his wife is going to remain.

Now he can begin to be the man she married and start concentrating on making her happy and doing more for her. Their friends and everyone they know will hear him boasting about the great wife he has. He will sing her praises at every opportunity. Can such a miraculous transformation happen in your man with such an easy concession? Yes! When a man feels loved by his wife, he will do everything in his power to make her happy.

Starting Over

Now that you have the information and understand the downward spiral in marriage and why it occurs, there is just one question you need to answer: Are you willing to do whatever it takes to turn your marriage around? Some women may feel so much damage has been done to the relationship that they can't possibly forgive their husband. Or perhaps they are already involved with another man and find themselves trapped in limbo between the two.

If you are involved with another man, you need to understand the truth about that relationship and realize you will get bored with him, too. Be realistic: What will you really gain by leaving your husband? You may wonder why I didn't pose this question to men, too. Remember, women are usually the ones who file for divorce. It is the wife who usually checks out emotionally from the marriage relationship.

If you decide to make your marriage work, you will not be disappointed by the results you achieve with just a few changes in behavior. I am not saying that this is going to be like flipping a light switch; it will take work on your part. Yet the rewards, oh the rewards! I believe they will be so plentiful for you!

Three Goals

1. Let It Go!

First, you need to recognize that no one can change the past. Second, realize your part even if it was unintentional. It was the normal decline in the female sex drive that drove your husband to attitudes and behaviors that you would have never experienced otherwise. Take a minute and think about this fact! If your drive had remained constant, or if you had the knowledge and understanding about marriage you have now, everything could have been different. He may have turned into a massive jerk, but he did not plan that, and everything would have been totally different if your drive had not dropped. Is it his fault his heart has been devastated repeatedly? You need to forgive him and let it go.

Think back to when you got married. What sort of man was he? How did he treat you? Did you marry a wonderful guy? I'm not asking about his behavior or actions since then. Did you marry a man you believed was wonderful? I'm betting you never would have married a man you didn't think was wonderful. That wonderful guy is still there and wants to live to make you happy again. Give him the chance!

I have spoken about the emotional replays that women experience. This may be one of the greatest obstacles you face in overcoming your situation. You will most likely find the old hurts resurface over and over again, rearing their ugly head and making you feel many different things toward your husband, none of them good. You can't stop emotional replays from resurfacing, but you can choose to let them go and not dwell on them or act on them. This is not just about forgiveness; this is about understanding and making peace in your marriage. If you're unwilling to confront your emotional replays with a plan to let them go, you may find it just about impossible to turn your husband around.

2. Return to the Woman of His Dreams

My wife and I reminisce often about the wonderful times we had during our courtship. So many moments and events felt magical to us. This is where you need to get your head and your heart. The goal now is to make him love you so deeply that the depth of your love for him will blow him away.

We have discussed the love actions and how we can control how much our partner loves us by making frequent, significant increases and few decreases. We have also discussed what's most important to men. You already know that every marriage needs an environment of affection. Whether he realizes it or not, he also needs you to provide an environment of affection towards him. He needs to see your kindness and gentleness again as he did during your courtship together.

When your husband begins to see these changes, he will start wondering what is going on. Men are not always the brightest bulb in the box, but we know when our woman is showing us love. Trust me when I tell you that providing he has not checked out emotionally, which few men do, he will respond to your changes and feel like he has the woman of his dreams back in his arms.

3. Understand and Accept Reality

He is not going to transform himself back into the man who courted you overnight. He will need time to see that what you are doing is genuine and that you are not going to take it away from him again. He has received a great deal of emotional pain from refusal and rejection, so turning the "love faucet" back on, so to speak, will be a huge change in his life.

You should start noticing positive changes in him fairly quickly, but that will not, in itself, make for a great marriage. You need to concentrate on pushing his love throttle to a higher position and helping him understand how to push yours.

Go back to the love actions section and write them down. Learn them, and then do them! Be an example to him. Sometimes men are a bit slow, but over time, we do get it and respond wonderfully when our wife loves us the way we need to be loved.

Also, you need to understand that when you give yourself to your husband, it may not be fireworks for you. But you must do it with sincere love and encourage him in the act. I'm not saying it won't be enjoyable for you, because it probably will be; just that it is not going to be like the peak of the sex the two of you used to have. You may have a period of adjustment as you begin having more sex. The adjustment normally takes about two weeks, but it could take up to a month before this becomes a habit that is easy to do. During the adjustment period, sex may not be wonderful, but according to the women with whom I've spoken, it gets incredibly better with time. Showing him love during each experience is important! In time, you will begin soaring in altitude as he begins to live to make you happy and loves doing it.

Orgasms

I am not going to go deep into this subject, because I am not a sex therapist, but you need to make certain he is giving you orgasms. Unfortunately, this is usually a tender area for the man. Many men do not understand that they do not have God-given natural gifts in the lovemaking area. Most men are open to suggestions and trying new things, so I would couch this as, "Let's experiment and try something different together."

If your husband is clueless about how to give you a G-spot orgasm, for example, he needs to educate himself. The G-spot orgasm is the most powerful and satisfying orgasm a woman can experience. Some women squirt while having a G-spot orgasm. Many women who have never been able to have a vaginal orgasm report achieving them after receiving a G-spot orgasm. Just about all women report that achieving a regular orgasm is far easier and far more pleasurable after experiencing a G-spot orgasm. G-spot orgasms can have a powerful effect on women! Once again, this subject needs to be handled delicately, because a man's ego is frail in this area. If you have not already had one, the G-spot orgasm is a wonderful orgasm for women, and every married man needs to learn how to do this for his wife. If your orgasms are more powerful and much easier to achieve, sex will be much more pleasurable for you, and engaging in intercourse will be something you look forward to doing.

Talk with Him About
What You Have Discovered

After you begin to give yourself to your husband regularly, ask him if you can spend some time together. Schedule it so there are no interruptions. Be loving towards him and cling to him. Treat him like you did when the two of you were courting. My wife clings to me just about everywhere we go. I'm not saying she never lets go, just that it is natural for her to have her arm wrapped in mine when we are walking together regardless of where we are. She holds my hand often when we go somewhere or are just sitting together. If you do this, he will begin to feel close to you and begin trusting his heart to you again when he sees this unending attitude of love from you.

Then explain what you have learned about the male and female sex drive. Let him know how you will be different in the future. My guess is he will glow with happiness, but even if he doesn't, don't let that deter you. What he has just learned about females may be very upsetting and he might not believe you will change. These heartaches can run deep!

Remember the woman from the man's enigma section that needed to talk and spend some quality time with her husband? He was rejecting her no matter how much or in what way she tried to approach him. This was emotionally devastating for her. Suppose the man in the example realized how much he was hurting his wife and decided never to treat her that way again. If this had been going on for months or years, do you think she would just accept he had changed because he told her so or because he started listening to her? Do you think she might be very careful emotionally by walking softly and slowly back into his affections? Would she not be on guard for any sign of insincerity? Wouldn't it take some time of consistency before she truly realized he had changed? This is probably how your husband will be as well! He has been devastated time and time again, so dropping his guard and really letting his heart begin trusting in you again may make him feel vulnerable. He might be watching for the smallest of actions or comments that show you are not sincere. Be careful and love him with all your heart every day and in time he will know you are back.

Continue to learn about him. Learn what you can do to help him feel loved. Once you have established a pattern of loving him and he knows you have made a real change, he will be thrilled again that he is married to you! He will likely come to you and ask what he can do to make you happy as well. If your husband does not make the first move, use quality time to explain that you need him to learn how to love you and make major increases in your love throttle.

Offer to read some parts of this book or the entire book to him. Many men hate to read but are happy to let their wife read to them. The more your husband understands the love throttle concept and how to make increases, the more you will see him going to great lengths to make sure you know how much he loves you. Once he begins to grasp these principles, and learns the love actions himself, you should see some major changes in his outlook and behavior towards you. Once both of your throttles are moving forward, your engines will be running on high again, and the two of you will soar with love and intimacy. Isn't that why you married him? Wasn't it your dream to have a beautiful love and life together? You know how to make that happen now, so do it!

A Challenge for Wives

As a woman, you may think I am wrong about this stuff, or you may be wondering if these things can possibly be true. If so, I have a challenge that will prove the truth of what I am telling you in this book. If you're married, I know I don't need to prove that your sexual desire for your husband has decreased; you live it every day. What I want to prove to you is the truth about men.

So, here's my challenge for wives who might be wondering if what I've said about husbands is true: Make love to your husband for the next thirty days. That's right, make love to him every day. There may be days when seduction is not required, as he may begin to come for it on his own. Regardless, make love to him for thirty days in a row. If your cycle comes, then resume as soon as it ends. Then behold the change in your man! Implement the love actions. Watch your actions transform him before your eyes into the loving and caring man who courted you. If I'm right, won't it be worth it to have your prince back again? Wouldn't it be worth the effort to have the man of your dreams loving you again? Think about how wonderful he used to be. He's still there waiting to be your prince!

Make certain you have a loving attitude of affection towards him as well. If you give him sex but then start complaining about something, it defeats the point of trying to show him you love him. Remember: the lovemaking is to make him feel you love him. Notice I said, "make him *feel*" you love him, not *know* it. There is a huge difference. Being loving and kind is a big part of this experiment. Do not disrespect him or belittle him during those thirty days. If you feel tempted, ask yourself this: How would it feel to see him adoring you again and making great efforts to make you happy?

Dr. Laura says repeatedly that men are simple creatures. When I heard her say this, at first, I was a bit insulted. The thing that aggravated me most was she was right. Willard F. Harley, Jr. says the number one need for a man is sex. Although this sounds shallow, it isn't when you understand that sex is a man's primary way of receiving love from his wife. Like my dad said: When a man has sex with his wife, he feels loved by her. There is nothing better in the world for a husband in love with his wife, than to feel his wife wrapped lovingly around him.

Give a man what he needs, and he will move mountains to please his wife. It is important that you do this with love and generosity each time, not begrudgingly or with a cavalier attitude. Use this time to teach him how to please you better. Learn and then show him how to give you a G-spot orgasm. For the first week or two, you may find this difficult. But it will get much easier, and you will likely see so much change in him you will not want to stop. During this time, you will begin enjoying lovemaking much more. Don't think so? Then take my challenge and prove me wrong! It's only thirty days, so what do you have to lose? Nothing, and you have a great deal to gain!

This is a win/win situation for women. They get to have a happy husband who wants to give them the world and great orgasms as well. Every wife needs this whether she realizes it or not. Don't think so? Then why are seventy percent of women unfaithful to their husbands? Why would any married woman end up in bed with a man other than her husband? Certainly no one can say it's because she has frequent sex and great orgasms with a husband that adores her! It doesn't take a brain surgeon to understand this. Women may not think they need regular sex, but the statistics say otherwise. Wives may not need sex as much as their husband, but they need it regularly, whether they feel like it or not.

Consider this as well: Why do women initiate up to ninety percent of divorces? Is this because all men are jerks? Think about this, ladies: Does any woman cheat because she's having too many orgasms with her spouse? Frequent sex is like a booster shot for the marriage each time it occurs. Frequent sex helps inoculate marriages against infidelity!

In the past, women gave the man how much he wanted, whenever he wanted it. In modern Western culture, women control relationships. That's just the way it is. For the most part, every woman has the marriage relationship she has created. Don't agree with me? Then try something different. Take my challenge and prove me wrong! I challenge you to see for yourself the power that is in your hands. Why not take my challenge and achieve wonderful and real intimacy with your man that will last forever? Remember the man with whom you fell in love? He's waiting for you.

If you refuse to take my challenge, don't complain about your husband to anyone when you refuse to do what every man needs from his wife to be happy. Plus, if at some point you do discover he is in an affair and in love with another woman, don't blame anyone but yourself! For the final time, I will refer you to a video by Dr. Laura. I just discovered all these videos, and I am so glad I did. Here is the link: https://www.youtube.com/watch?v=WOu0Z1hkxp0.

What If He's Having an Affair?

When a wife begins to make changes in her love life and attitude towards her husband, it is possible she might discover her husband is having an affair and is even in love with another woman. If this is the case, his affair partner has been making huge increases in his most important area while the wife has been making huge decreases. If this happens to you, consider this: Are you willing to forgive your husband, meet his needs, and put in the effort required to end his affair? This affair is his responsibility, but if he has been getting little to no sex, you should be able to understand why he is getting it from someone else.

If the answer is *yes,* you need to let him know that although what he did was horribly wrong, you realize how important his need for sex is. Then you need to promise not to withhold sex from him ever again. He will most likely test you by taking you over and over again! One good thing is that most men do not leave the marriage relationship willingly in an emotional sense. He will most likely agree to end the affair providing you are willing to do your part in the marriage from now on.

Next, you need all the details about how they meet. Your husband must be willing to disclose any secret methods of communicating and meeting with the affair partner. If the affair partner is in a place where he encounters her every day, such as at work, he has to search for a new job. He will not be able to stay away from a woman he loves when he is around her regularly! He needs your help to break free. A husband might even be afraid to admit he loves the other woman and lie about it, but if he cannot break free from her, most likely he does love her.

This process requires total openness. There should be no privacy from your spouse in marriage anyway! You will need passwords to his email, cell phone, Facebook, everything. You also need the other woman's phone number and address and email address. You need to let him know you will be checking these accounts. He needs to call or write and break it off with the woman in front of you.

Next, he needs to understand he no longer has the freedom to be anywhere without you knowing where he is and being able to verify his location. You need to use a GPS app like "Where's my Droid" or "Apple GPS" on his smart phone, and only you should have the password to it. This will allow you to text the app, which will reply with coordinates on a Google map, and he will not even know you did it. You need to use it so he understands you know how to find him and will attempt to do so from time to time. This surveillance needs to continue for eighteen months to two years.

Some women may be thinking: *If I can't trust him, what's the point?* This is not about trust; this is about helping him break free from his love addiction to the affair partner. Consider this: The addiction never would have happened if his wife had kept her part of the sacred trust agreement.

One wife I know even involved her husband's family. She confessed her part in the failure of the marriage, and his family agreed to support her. They turned on him and let him know that as long as his wife genuinely loved him, no other woman would ever be accepted or welcomed into his family or into their home. This additional family pressure helped him to break free from his affair partner, because the cost was too high. That was several years ago, and the couple is still happily married today. They have children, and he is a devoted husband and father.

He's Not Interested in Sex

If your husband is not interested in sex with you, you have a serious problem on your hands. There are only a few possible explanations. First, have you made major changes to your appearance so that he no longer sees you as beautiful? Just ask him, "Why don't you desire me? Have I changed my appearance so much you don't find me attractive anymore?" If this is his problem, and he is honest enough to admit it, you need to start getting back to your old self.

He may have a "mommy complex" with you. This can occur with men whose father was absent or passive in his relationship with his wife. The mother was left with most of the responsibilities, and she had some issues where the son was more the husband to her (even though there may not have been any sex) than the father. The problem requires counseling that is outside the scope of this book. This is well known in psychiatry, and there is a great deal of help available.

Another possibility is an addiction to porn. A porn addiction can be worse than cocaine. Over time, a man will need to ramp it up more and more. Should you discover your husband has a porn addiction, I recommend professional help, as he will likely never break free without it. This type of behavior is very destructive to a marriage.

It's also possible he has fallen in love with another woman. If this is the case, I have already explained what to do providing he has not left the marriage emotionally.

It is also possible he was molested as a young child or young man and may have some serious issues for which he will need to receive counseling. Once again, you need to get him to open up to you about why he does not want sex with you.

The final possibility is one that I have encountered several times. He may be bisexual or gay, and he may have a male lover. Unfortunately, women make it easy for married men to get away with this behavior. First, his wife may be happy not to have sex with him, so he is free to put all of his efforts into the other man. In addition, his wife probably thinks nothing about him hanging out with a friend for sports or other activities. This is great cover for their affair together, since the wife is clueless due to her own failure to consider it as a possibility. Gay men will do this when they want friends and family to believe they are straight. They will marry for cover, and the wife unwittingly helps to maintain this cover by withdrawing sexually, which gives him complete freedom with his lover.

12

SOME OTHER ITEMS OF PARAMOUNT IMPORTANCE FOR INTIMACY

Some problems do not fall into the previous chapters, but they are still important. Here are a few situations to avoid and things to avoid doing.

People get frustrated, and every marriage will have problems to solve. This book has concentrated on problems common to most marriages but which are not known or understood. I believe that when a couple has genuine intimacy, they can tackle just about any problem together and find a workable solution.

There are pitfalls to avoid that help a great deal in getting along with each other and protecting your intimacy and love together. Something you need to decide is when it's time to elevate an issue to the point of an argument.

His Eyes Wander

Women fail often to understand the basic nature of men. We are extremely visual, and there's not a thing we can do about it. Many men are frustrated and embarrassed by this instinctual behavior. When a man sees a woman who is beautiful or dressed provocatively, he can't help but look at her. Now, I am not speaking about standing there gawking with our tongues hanging out; that is different. But a woman in a short skirt, displaying cleavage, or dressed in some other provocative way is always going to draw your husband's eyeballs. She might just be a beautiful woman, but he has no control. It has nothing to do with your man in particular. It's the way all men are wired. Sometimes we hate ourselves for this. You need to realize this is not because he desires anyone besides you; he doesn't! Don't get angry over something he has not done on purpose.

Case in point: My wife and I went on a cruise on Lake Michigan recently. The cruise lasted about two hours. It was a large sailboat, and the ship was crowded.

We sat down, and twenty-four inches across from us was a couple. The woman was pretty and had on an extremely short skirt. When she sat down, she needed to keep her legs together constantly. This was a bit of a struggle for me. For one thing, my eyes kept returning to those legs. It was highly embarrassing. What if my wife, or the woman, caught me looking? I tried to keep my eyes away from her, but when she moved or repositioned herself, I found myself looking up to see what was happening.

Then it happened: Her legs were open, and I had a clear view. For the rest of the cruise, I kept my eyes shut! Noticing my eyes were shut, Paula asked if I was okay.

"Yes," I replied, "but the woman in front of us is dressed so scantily that I can't keep from looking, so I'm just going to keep my eyes closed for the rest of the cruise."

For me, this was the right thing to do out of respect for my Sweet Paula. Paula has never been upset because my eyes are drawn to another woman. She knows how much I love her and that this is a natural struggle for men. I want women to understand this is about male instincts, not a wandering husband. It is in our DNA. Ladies, please understand that this is difficult for your husband, and cut him a little slack. There is no reason to get jealous or upset, so don't be angry or hurt. One more thing: Keep in mind the effect you have on men by the way you dress.

Choose Your Battlefield Carefully

Just because someone is frustrated or upset does not mean an argument must follow. There are times when you or your partner will feel different strains and pressures in life. The pressures may have nothing to do with anything either of you has done. Your partner could be venting because of some problem unrelated to you or your marriage. If this is the case, don't take it personally. Let your partner vent. He or she will feel better, and it will not have any effect on your relationship.

At other times, your partner might create pressure in the marriage. Your partner may reach a point where he or she becomes so frustrated that he or she is unable to communicate in a spirit of love. We are all human. Your partner may unload on you, or you may unload on your partner. When this happens, it's best for the spouse under attack to take it in and not respond in a negative way.

Let your partner express his or her frustrations, and then give it some thought for a while. If your spouse looks for a response, just let him or her know you want time to process what was said. This allows both of you time to think about the remarks without losing control over something that might end up being meaningless. Only after you have taken the time to process it carefully and without malice should you respond. This also gives your partner time to think about how he or she feels as well.

You may find that while you are taking time to process what was said that your spouse comes to regret saying it and apologizes. This happens more often than not. What if you had flown off the handle at your spouse in response to the issue and engaged in a full-throttled argument?

If, after some time thinking about it, you agree with your spouse, let your spouse know you have considered the issue and that your spouse is right. If an apology is appropriate, apologize. However, if you feel your spouse is wrong, explain why you think this is the case. Once again, keep things calm and loving. If your partner disagrees, the two of you will need to decide to whom it is most important. Avoid the Battle of Hamburger Hill at all costs!

The Battle Of Hamburger Hill[20]

During the Vietnam War, American commanders determined they needed to take Hill 937,

---

[20] The following is an edited and revised version of the Wikipedia account: https://en.wikipedia.org/wiki/Battle_of_Hamburger_Hill

which was occupied by the North Vietnamese. The hill was heavily fortified, but the order was given to take the hill anyway.

US forces made a full frontal assault on the hill for ten days beginning May 10, 1969. The battle was primarily an infantry engagement, with US troops moving up the steep hill against well entrenched enemy troops. The North Vietnamese defense repelled the attacks repeatedly. Bad weather also hindered operations. Nevertheless, the airborne troops took the hill through direct assault, causing extensive casualties to both sides.

US losses during the 10-day battle totaled 72 American and 372 friendly troops. To take the position, the 101st Airborne Division eventually committed five infantry battalions and ten batteries of artillery. In addition, the Air Force flew an additional 272 missions and expended more than 500 tons of ordnance.

US estimates of the losses incurred by the enemy totaled 630 dead (discovered on and around the battlefield), including many found in makeshift mortuaries within the tunnel complex. Yet, no one could count the number of the enemy running off the mountain. Then there were those killed by artillery and air-strikes, the wounded and dead carried into Laos, or the dead buried in collapsed bunkers and tunnels.

After the battle was over, commanders determined the hill had no real strategic value and abandoned it. This battle was a waste of blood, money, and resources. We need to make certain when we choose to plant our personal flag in the ground, the hill is worth the cost of taking it. Too many times couples engage in senseless arguments over issues that are not of any real importance. Make certain that if you are willing to go to battle for an issue, you have exhausted all peaceful attempts to resolve the matter and it is worth the cost.

Don't Hit Below the Belt

Marriage gives people particular insight into their spouse's weakest areas. You need to make certain when there is a disagreement, no one fights below the belt or with disrespect for the other person. When you have a legitimate issue, your partner knows it. Even if they disagree, they respect your position. When you belittle your partner, you show disrespect and pull back on his or her love throttle. Furthermore, you destroy intimacy by violating the sacred trust. After all, belittling your partner is often taking things only you know about them and then turning those things against him or her.

You might be right, but how you convey yourself might cause you to lose the battle. When you treat your partner with disrespect, you're demeaning his or her character. This is the love of your life! This is your lifelong sweetheart. You are destroying the person you love the most in life. How do you expect your partner is going to respond to being demeaned? Your partner will feel so upset there is no way you are going to walk away feeling good after the exchange.

If you have a legitimate issue, it will stand on its own merits, and there's no reason to involve any disagreement from the past. When you belittle your partner, you lose the moral high ground, and your issue looks to be of little importance compared with how you are dealing with it.

Discuss things in a loving manner even when you are upset. If you can't talk rationally, wait until you can before you engage your partner in discussion.

Do Not Allow Anyone Other Than Your Spouse to Make Love Throttle Increases!

"No flirting" is a rule to be observed by both husband and wife. Remember that affairs begin innocently. When you allow anyone other than your spouse to make love throttle increases, you are violating your vow to let your spouse alone meet your most personal needs. Praise should only be allowed from your partner. It is a love action.

We all run into people who say flattering words from time to time. The problem begins when a person of the opposite sex begins making regular compliments or listens to your personal problems. Many people believe in "harmless flirting." Flirting tells a person you find him or her attractive and that you have chemistry with them. If they find you attractive as well, an affair could start very easily whether you want to believe it or not. This can even happen if you are happily married. Many might disagree with me, but they are wrong! Women need to be particularly careful to not respond with body language when a good-looking man throws them a compliment. The best thing to do is to ignore the compliment. Protect your marriage!

Should you come across someone who keeps it up, you need to address the person directly about it and let him or her know you do not want his or her compliments. Just explain you are happily married to the greatest spouse in the world and do not want to be rude, but you don't care what anyone besides your spouse thinks of you. The person may feel a bit embarrassed, but he or she will move on.

Never discuss your problems with the opposite sex. This can open doors that need to stay shut. Although it might be innocent and you may have no ulterior motives, things can spiral out of control before you realize it. If you need to talk to someone other than your spouse, talk to a friend of the same sex.

Finally, avoid eye contact with the opposite sex. This is body language that telegraphs you are interested in them.

Sex vs. Loving Who Your Partner Is

When two people begin having sex before they get to know each other, and the sex is good, they usually will develop deep feelings for each other quickly. The woman is generally first to feel this, but in time, the man also develops similar feelings. If the man is having sex with more than one woman, he will not develop feelings of love, but she will. How do you know if he has more honeys on the side? You have no way to know this short of hiring a private detective, and few people will do that.

Many friends in my youth talked about "stage-five clingers," women they had slept with and abandoned for someone else. The women continued to pursue them though, because these women believed they were in love with the man. This man often tells his friends, "I hardly even know her; we just slept together a few times." Although it is less often, men can develop feelings for a woman who has multiple partners. The result is the same, but this time he is the one with feelings. How humiliating for a woman or a man who puts themselves in such a position.

If there is no one else, their love may continue to grow, providing they have good chemistry together. This is often the case with affair sex as well. The problem is, feelings are based on chemistry and not on knowing the other person. If this couple gets married, how will she feel towards him when she begins to lose her desire for him? Now this couple has to try to build real love and intimacy together.

This is why I did not kiss my Sweet Paula until we had said, "I love you" to each other. We fell in love with each other through getting to know each other, not through getting physical with each other.

If you are a couple that started with sex, your battle to achieve intimacy is not impossible as long as you maintain respect for each other. Couples throughout the history of the world have achieved real love and intimacy even though they had not met before marriage. However, it takes a lot more work as you begin to get to know and love the actual person you married.

Painful Intercourse and Menopause

Some women who have gone through menopause may find sex to be painful. This is usually because of vaginal atrophy. If you find intercourse painful, see a doctor, especially before taking me up on my thirty-day challenge. Using hormone cream for a few weeks will usually solve this problem.

Women may also experience some drop in libido after menopause due to the loss of female hormones. Many women report great success with natural remedies. You may also need to see your doctor for other options that are available to women after menopause.

CONCLUSION

I have limited the subject matter discussed in this book to what I believe is critical to having a wonderful and intimate marriage. That doesn't mean there's not a great deal more to understand about women and men in marriage. This book could have easily been twice the length, but I believe it had to be limited in scope so more people will read it. Larger books are daunting, and it's harder to find the time to read them. All that to say, don't stop here. Read more and continue learning about your spouse.

It is my sincere hope and prayer that this book will serve as a marriage manual that will give people the knowledge they need to bring genuine love and intimacy back into their marriage. I believe that if you apply the information in this book to your marriage, it will be bulletproof against affairs, which is the leading cause of divorce.

My heart breaks when I see the state of marriage today. It breaks even more when I see God loving people who were in love, filing for divorce because one spouse has had an affair. We all want happy marriages. The problem is, most of us don't understand what caused such despair in our marriages.

When I was a pastor, too often people came into my office and announced they were getting a divorce. My first question to the person each time was this: Who is he or she? I knew there was almost always an affair partner.

Everyone wants to be loved and adored by his or her spouse. Apply the principles and methods you have learned in this book, and make it happen for you and your partner!

Ask yourself this question: If seventy-two percent of men and seventy percent of women cheat, what is the total percentage of marriages that have infidelity? This is a sobering thing to consider.

It is my sincere desire that you will learn from my heartfelt journey for truth and apply the solutions for these enigmas which break hearts and often, cause affairs. I believe God has revealed them to me. I have no other explanation for gaining the knowledge in this book other than God revealing this truth so I can share it with others.

I wish there had been a book like this for me to read when I was a younger man. The principles and methods laid out here have helped me to have the best relationship of my life. My wife and I love and adore each other every day of our lives. We live by and use the principles and methods in this book, and it has made our marriage nothing short of spectacular. The honeymoon has never ended for us, and I want that for you as well. Our love is stronger and our intimacy deeper today then the day we got married. I believe it can be that way for you, too!

Take the information you have learned in this book and make your marriage soar with love and intimacy! Now you know how to do that. Show your partner that he or she has the love of his or her life, that wonderful person your spouse dreamed of marrying, back in his or her arms adoring them again. Your life will never be the same, and your marriage will be an example to your children, friends, and family.

Made in the USA
Middletown, DE
27 May 2016